tiger heart,
tiger mind

Other Zentrepreneur Guides® by Ron Rubin and
Stuart Avery Gold:

Success at Life: How to Catch and Live Your Dream

Dragon Spirit: How to Self-Market Your Dream

Wowisms: Words of Wisdom for Dreamers and Doers

Also by Ron Rubin and Stuart Avery Gold

Tea Chings: The Tea and Herb Companion

NEWMARKET PRESS
New York

tiger heart, tiger mind

How to Empower Your Dream

RON RUBIN AND STUART AVERY GOLD

MINISTERS OF  The REPUBLIC of TEA

First Edition
1-55704-621-2 (hardcover)

10   9   8   7   6   5   4   3   2   1

Interior art by Machiko

Cover art by Gina Amador

Library of Congress Cataloging-in-Publication Data

Rubin, Ron, 1949-
  Tiger heart, tiger mind : how to empower your dream : a Zentrepreneur's guide / Ron Rubin and Stuart Avery Gold. —1st ed.
    p. cm.
Includes bibliographical references and index.
ISBN 1-55704-621-2 (hardcover : alk. paper)
1. Success—Psychological aspects. I. Gold, Stuart Avery. II. Title.
BF637.S8R785 2004
158—dc22

2004003508

QUANTITY PURCHASES
Companies, professional groups, clubs, and other organizations may qualify for special terms when ordering quantities of this title. For information, write Special Sales, Newmarket Press, 18 East 48th Street, New York, NY 10017, call (212) 832-3575, fax (212) 832-3629, or e-mail mailbox@newmarketpress.com.

www.newmarketpress.com

Manufactured in the United States of America.
At the authors' request, this book has been printed on acid-free paper.

For the kids

~.~

This is my simple religion.

There is no need for temples;

no need for complicated philosophy.

Our own brain,

our own heart is our temple.

—The Dalai Lama

Contents

Chapter One
SO FEW ARE THE MANY

The heart allows that which the mind can only dream.

Ghosts forever.

Where once one hundred thousand wondrous wild tigers regally roamed the humid jungles and dense hardwood forests of Asia, it is now estimated that fewer than four thousand of the magnificent awe-inspiring creatures are left. And you must know what madness is being perpetrated on them—and this is important—these remaining noble few continue to spiral tragically into extinction at the hands of man. The concern is immediate. The World Wide Fund for Nature has sized up the situation and claims that tigers are disappearing at the horrendous rate of one every day. And if there are any among you who are capable of hurling down lightning bolts from heaven, you should not suppress the sense of outrage at the wiping out of these grand and glorious beasts, nor should you hold back your sadness at their shattering disappearance. Because as they vanish, so too fades the spirit and the light that for thousands of years long the tiger has symbolized.

The ancients believed that the tiger represented the true heart and true mind of the instinctual self. The ancients indicated that we human beings could hold the same timeless dominion. That like the tiger, we too possess an innate capacity to transform mental and emotional energy into physical energy. That like the tiger, we too have an ability to unleash the hidden power of our heart and mind so that we may journey a life full of confidence and beauty. And that like the tiger, we too are forever and always this:

More than what we seem.

For millennia, the Chinese have observed the cosmic breath that pervades all of life, the spiritual knot between mankind and nature. Picking up from below, taking from above, they concluded that when all living things are allowed to go their own way, the universe experiences an existence of order, harmony, and abundance. This is the Chinese principle of *hsiang sheng* or mutual arising. That all things and all beings are interrelated and mutually interdependent upon each other for existence. That everything has a place in the natural order, that one thing cannot exist without the other. Without darkness there is no light. Without stillness there is no movement. Without silence there is no sound. You exist for the world and the world exists for you. The masters suggested that to deny this is to deny the existence of the entire universe. But choose to embrace this and the whole universe surrenders to your greatest dream, what the Chinese call *hsing*.

Your heart-mind . . .

Your own true nature . . .

Your destiny.

There is a celebrated Zen parable about a master who was asked about the highest teaching of Zen. What is the wellspring of a happy and contented life? In quietude, the sage master scratched the character for the word "Attention" in the sand. There must be something else, his student asked. Yes, there is, replied the master and he again scribed the sand with the character for "Attention." But is there not something more, questioned the student. Yes, and here the master paused a moment before he once again marked the sand with the character for "Attention." Now the sand exalted, "Attention. Attention. Attention."

What you must know is this . . . attention is the price we pay for a fulfilled life. If you want to live your best life, be prepared to pay the price. And what you must believe is this . . . attention must be paid to our undernourished ability to connect heart and mind. To do so is to empower the ultimate spirit of the tiger, experiencing the expansive sense of intuition, confidence, and contentment.

So few are the many who realize that by empowering ourselves to awaken the way within, we can travel to a higher level of awareness, another level of consciousness, where guided by the heart, nurtured by the mind, we are able to transcend circumstance, delivering ourselves from nightmares of our own making to the grand and glorious dreams waiting to have us. How sad that many of our fellowship have become lost in the wretched woes of hurrying to experience a better life when the real wonder of life is in the experience itself. The French novelist and memoir-writer Colette said, "What a wonderful life I have had. I only wish I had realized it sooner." And let me add this—my favorite: a beginner asks the elder monk, "Is there anything more miraculous than the wonders of our lives?" The elder monk answers, "Yes, your awareness of the wonders of our lives."

One of the great truths is to live a life of happiness we must be awake to the sacredness of what we are and what we can do—the infinite opportunities and possibilities that await us if we pay attention to each and every moment and live in a fully conscious manner. Appreciate how extraordinary life is, in and of itself. Feel gratitude. Practice awareness for the wonder of our lives, because life itself is filled with wonder. Without such marvel and exuberance, our hopes and dreams will sag, amounting to nothing.

Grab hold the process of discovery and immersion, that's the message that matters. Allow yourself to realize your grandest potential. If you want each new day that dawns to greet you with a nod of sunshine, mindfulness must be given to your glories, your inborn talents, gifts, virtues, and abilities. Realize, please, complacency is not part of your organic pattern, greatness is. No need to seek out any egghead scientist to inquire if a gene splice can make this an add-on option. It's already here, inside each and everyone of us, waiting to be claimed. Like the tiger, greatness is more than a smidgen of our DNA—it's the spine of our genetic makeup that, when seized, will guide us to the lives we were meant to live. Sadly, it's our fear of engaging our greatness that haunts our dreams the most.

And keeps us from realizing our best life.

The operative term in that sentence is best life. Understand something—there is nothing elusive about your ability to turn your most desired dream into a living reality. It is your birthright, an endowment given you once you stop searching outside for answers that lie within. Joseph Campbell stated, "The goal of life is to make your heartbeat match the beat of the universe. To match your nature with nature." Not a challenging charge, if you would only embrace the grace that is yours to do and to be. Dive deeply into being. Devour bliss. Surrender to your true calling. Engage your want to's. Living the life you imagine is not something to be acquired by outer means, rather it is a total awakening to the capacity of your own true nature that is the start of everything.

And makes life magic.

Now, as those of you who have joined us on previous excursions know, not too many pages get to go by without Ron and me devoting some ink on paper to a discussion concerning our euphoric love of tea. We are mad about tea. Can't get enough of it to quiet our addiction. Next to good old aqua pura, the nectar of the leaf is civilization's oldest beverage, an ancient friend to both body and mind, a true tonic heralded for its illustrious history, its comfort, its serenity, its healthful benefits, the thousand pleasures that it provides between the first sip and the last. Simply said, tea has given us a way to work in a way that takes care of what's truly important. Our self-imposed indenture to its tranquil spell and haunting boundlessness has taken us on a journey of many cups. Tea has been a world of light, our passport to adventure to faraway frontiers. Once outsiders, Ron and I have become insiders, trekking over earth that has never held the feet of a Westerner. We have been privileged to experience a cultural synthesis of sweeping scope and high ideals, vital connectives that have requited us with a newly honed appreciation for the human journey, the profound essence of which no one can characterize, although the sages have come close, calling it "the way."

The practice of our best self.

By using the word way, what we are invoking is the spiritual dimension of the Chinese word *tao* and the Japanese word *do*, both of which mean path or way—a holistic, transcendent concept. Interpreted not as a road or trail, but as an integrating dynamism—a method, principle, or doctrine that when practiced, results in perfecting one's higher self, physically, mentally, and spiritually. To try and grasp a better understanding of this is to try and grasp a better understanding of the ancient principle that is at the very center of the study and application of *chado*—the Way of Tea, or *chanoyu*—the tea ceremony, a skill that requires an artistic ability of awareness that even after years of painstaking perpetual practice, you will find yourself off to only a solid start.

To study the centuries-old Japanese discipline of

chanoyu is to study the art of life, where such concepts as harmony, respect, purity, tranquility, and above all else, the life artistry of awareness, where one's heart and one's mind are polished and reflected upon, become a way of revealing to ourselves who we truly are. This artful practice is total, toward all of one's existence, not just to the existence that takes place in the tearoom. It is a powerful metaphor for how we view the world and our experiences in it.

Plus this, the Way of Tea delivers the sipper out of a hyperactive weary world of rush, din, and everyday sameness to a place of peace and contentment. A reflective state where contentment leads directly to the sanctuary of the subtle and silent, the consciousness of inner content—here between the youth of the water and the poetry of the leaf, openness and wonder truly exist. Where we can stop and quietly listen and find our grandest potential. For we have known a cup of tea can do just that, to provide the calm and clarity that allows for the communion with ourself so we can be open to asking the right question. After all, too much of life is spent looking for the right answers, when in fact the secret to life lies in being able to ask the right questions. Truth to tell, it is the questions we ask, or fail to ask, that shape our path. And so the Way of Tea invites us all to become one with "the way," to bring the practice of mindfulness to all aspects of our life. Like any practice, the way is not a thing to be conquered, but rather it is an ongoing process that ennobles fully what you are capable of.

To live a life ecstatic.

Please believe we know one thing for sure. Right now, at this moment, you can realize the greatness of your dream by simply possessing the unwavering confidence to realize the greatness of your self. Look, turning your fondest dream into a living reality has nothing to do with your race, genes, fate, or luck. It does, however, have everything to do with your willingness to learn the wisdom of true knowledge anew, affirming the richness of your life with the unified concept of purposeful action and wisdom.

Tiger heart, tiger mind.

This book is about waking up every morning of the world with a will and a willingness to practice doing and being. A Zentrepreneur's Guide of information and inspiration on how to actively take responsibility for your life and make the most of it by resolving to manifest your dream into reality. Because that is what a Zentrepreneur is: someone who endeavors to study and practice, to live a life where the creative spark, the inner illumination of an open heart and initiating mind is put into motion, fostering growth that not only enriches one's own life, but the lives of others as well. But more than that, a

Zentrepreneur is someone who has made his or her life rich beyond counting by living a dream defined.

Pssst ... keep in mind this releasing truth: *While entrepreneurs are remembered for having a dream, Zentrepreneurs are remembered for allowing the dream to have them.*

It is our grand hope that these pages will be put to use and not just read. That you will employ them as your trusted companion for a pilgrimage of practice and expansion, a charted path of lessons and learnings that will surround and deliver you beyond the horizon to new vistas, insights, and unlimited possibilities. A journey of enlightenment, encouragement, and reassurance that can awaken the way within and move you ever onward, empowering you to experience the WOWs and wonders of your so richly deserved dream. A guided encounter with your own capacity to rechannel your passion, abundance, and grace into a dynamic new energy that can strengthen the will of your heart and polish the power of your mind. And how can we know with such certainty this book will do as we say?

Shhhh ... Because we have secrets.

All Zentrepreneurs do. And one of the most closely kept is that still and forever during our entire life on earth, each and every one of us gets to have two lives. There's the one we learn with, and then there's the life we live with after that.

Can't ask for more ...

—*Stuart Avery Gold*

Chapter Two
DARE TO DREAM, DREAM TO DARE

CREATE AN IDEA LOG

Never awaken a sleeping tiger.

This book began because of a poem.

Ever since I was a small bit, I have derived delight from the beauty that exists in the form and formlessness of literary verse composition. I have in all ways found fascinating how brilliantly a poem, this song of the soul, can articulate the power of a compassionate heart and unhindered mind. The ability to put words down in a particular way that may meet the eye and voice, a telling that locks the poet and the reader into a shared realization, is a huge weapon for any poet and one that writers spend their lives panting to possess. However, since most of my time in lit class was spent staring from my seat close to the window, to this day I haven't too much of a handle on the definition of difference between a lyric, sonnet, limerick, or rhyme. Still I absorbed much of the good stuff. As an aside, I liked John

Donne's "No man is an island, entire of itself; every man is a piece of the continent, a part of the main...." I adored Robert Frost's "Whose woods these are I think I know. His house is in the village, though...." And then there's the one that gave me more pleasure than anything else at the time, mine and every ten-year-old boy's fave—Edgar P. and his terrific "Once upon a midnight dreary, while I pondered, weak and weary...." So, like I said, as my memory offers, I did absorb a lot of the good stuff despite my being seated next to the staring window. And I tell you this because again, circling back, this book began because of a poem—the words of which belong to Carl Sandburg. His following line is truly one of the salvations of my life and one that still echoes:

"Nothing happens unless first a dream."

Now let me recite that again for those of you who are new to the Zentrepreneur concept:

"Nothing happens unless first a dream."

Please cling to that truth. Because in order to create a fulfilling future, you must first envision or dream it. Dreams are your creative vision, a way to explore, expand, and redefine the infinite possibilities of your life. They are an invitation to dance enthusiastically with your ideal future. Too often people look desperately outside their lives for what they want, when the creative power to build their best life lies within. By consciously directing yourself to the realm of your subconscious, your deep intuitive knowing, you give your soul self-permission to visualize your dream desire. Doing this, you become an agent for positive transformation and change, because dreams can provide us all with a fabulous sense of purpose and direction as well as the mental and emotional energy needed to empower ourselves and our lives.

Now, of course, before we go any further, it's important that you understand the difference between a dream and a fantasy. Winning the lottery, getting a call from a pleading Cameron Diaz asking you to run away with her, or that out-of-some-blue, knock-on-the-door visit from Brad Pitt, where he explains it was all a mistake and that it's you who he really loves and needs, that's fantasy. By dream, we mean rising to a higher level than the beddy-bye slumber kind. What we are talking about here is the wide-eyed genus of dream that will keep you up late and get you up early. A creative awakening of powerful inspirational vision that reveals the truth of your existence and imbues and propels you with inexhaustible energy, excitement, and motivation. A dream is your creative vision, the great idea for your life that when discovered becomes very much urgent, making your heart go pitty-pat faster and faster until that golden day you decide to claim it and make it real. In other words, fantasy is using your creative imagination as an escape from reality, while dreams engage your creative imagination to transform your reality.

Caution. Once you understand that dreams are not fantasies, but possibilities, you must also understand that a dream can easily shape shift into a fantasy, unless you make a deliberate, conscious, persistent effort to go along with it and turn it into a reality. Realize, here and now, that to live a dream delighted is not some rare privilege handed only to others who are more gifted, luckier, or more advantaged then you. It is the primal birthright belonging to every man and woman that does not resist discovery of the ocean of bliss, realizing that to enter the stream of happiness, you have simply to flow with it.

Create the uncreated. Hand-over-heart promise yourself to dream only the biggest dreams. The bigger you dream, the more creative energy you will put into achieving your dream. Creative energy is the currency required to fund fulfillment and allow you to experience the joy of being fully alive. Resolve to have the volition to say YES to the courage and confidence to live the life that you were meant to live. Dare to dream. Dream to dare. Be bold. Let your imagination proffer possibilities and ignite your passions. Allow WOW. Blow off black and white. Ground out gray. Destroy dull and drab. Dream with vibrant veracity. Tom Peters, the world's most thought-provoking guru to greatness extols that life demands Technicolor ideas and Technicolor actions. He's right. Very right. Commit yourself to a journey of intense imaginative exploration. Imagination is the conduit for creativity. Creativity gives birth to the great idea for your life, as well as the actions that will give rise to right circumstances that will empower you to consecrate your innate talents, unique gifts, and awesome natural abilities.

But the dream has to be your own.

If there is one clear direction Ron and I can give you to set your compass on the right path, that is it. The unspeakable great tragedy of our times is that all too many give themselves over to the pleasing of others in hopes of gaining approval or avoiding disapproval. They put off pursuing their own dreams, languishing in the litany of woulda-shoulda-coulda. Worse. Squandering their talents and gifts. Worse yet. Relinquishing the decision-making power of who they truly are and what they want to do over to someone else.

Now we don't know everything, but what we absolutely do know is this: Living life externally, where what others think, say, and do becomes the basic pulse of influence that rules the day, is an oblivion too bleak to bear. To mention nothing of the awful despair. How sad for them. But how about you? Do you practice freedom of mind? Are you able to see deeply into the nature of existence and understand what glories await you when you decide from inside? This empowerment is available to you at every moment, without exception. You need only to choose to ignore the pressure placed upon you by others. In other great words, "To thine own self be true." Are you? Think about it please. Are you in fact, living your life or are you living someone else's? Take a few seconds while we move ahead a little to put down something crucial enough to warrant bigger ink. Ready for it?

YOU MATTER!
YOUR DREAMS MATTER!

And it's the living of your own dream that very much matters the most. Your dream is your certain significant gift to mankind. It's the creative vehicle through which you are able to deliver your best in order to transform reality, helping to make this blue marble we all inhabit a better place on which to graze. True, you are convinced that some time in the future you will figure out a way to get the permission of those around you to go after your dream. True, in your heart of hearts you believe that some day you will be able to make the time to accomplish your dream. To that we say, not good enough. You cannot—you must not—spend your life peeking between the curtains, hoping somehow you'll have a happy ending. Stop waiting for permission! When you were born the cutting of the umbilical cord was your life-long permission to be yourself. Wait not. You have but only one opportunity to be you and your life is it. In the great grand scheme of things, our lives are but a blink of an eye and none of us knows when that blink will occur. This last point needs a bit of pausing over because, as we all know by now, evil does exist on Earth and tomorrow is promised to no one.

Don't sentence yourself to being a pleaser, there's no law. You simply must not put your dreams up on a shelf in order to satisfy others. You owe it to yourself. To us. To the citizenship of the world as a whole. It's the reason you are here as a card-carrying member of the human race. The cost of the membership: your obligation to discover and manifest your unique purpose and mission in life and set it free. Dante said, "A mighty flame followeth a tiny spark." Look around you—everything you see, every convenience of daily living we use and ultimately take for granted, all the technology, ritual, books, art, music, and entertainment we enjoy, began as a dawning, an inspiration, a creative vision that existed as a result of someone's imagination and intuition. From the very beginning since our primitive ancestors first thought of using fire to flicker the darkness to Edison's dream of the electric light bulb, the capacity for creative vision has been latent inside each and every one of us, waiting to be welcomed. At the end, it is your discovery of the important vision for your life and your ardent courage and determination to follow it through that are the beginnings of everything.

But how to start? How do you create the results you seek and live a life with full heart and elated mind? How do you go about amply acquiring and possessing the vision to see all the possibilities that can elevate ordinary existence to the level of sublime delight? How do you discover your wellspring of precious blessings and bring them into being? Easy answer—

By doing nothing.

Now before you throw the book across the room, please let us explain what we mean. By doing nothing, what we would like to bring here to our party is the purifying, ages-old Chinese concept of *wu-wei*, which literally means "doing-not doing." No mind-boggling babble to be confused with idleness or laziness, this Taoist principle is actually a profound, lo, very, very subtle thing. It is an ineffable silence. A stillness within activity and an activity within stillness. A state of actionless action in which the individual reaches an ability to give rise to actions that are acutely intuitive and correct through intense, intrinsic concentration.

To help understand this further is to understand the timeless teachings of inspiration and absorption that Chinese artists gave to their novice students. "Meditate on bamboo until you become bamboo, then paint yourself." By entering what they paint, to the point where they themselves dissolve, the inner life and aesthetic beauty of the object will be expressed effortlessly through their hands in deft, intuitive strokes. Moving ahead a few thousand years, when the very great master Louis Armstrong was asked how he came to play his style of jazz, he answered. "I don't. It plays me."

Musicians call it being in the groove, athletes call it the zone, artists call it the flow, a Zentrepreneur calls it a luminous state of awareness. Now we can use all the ink on paper in the world to go on about *wu-wei*, but it can never be meaningfully described, alas, it can ultimately be comprehended only through the actual experience (try to explain the taste of a plum to someone who has never tasted a plum). The simplest praise that can be sung for *wu-wei* is that it calls for inaction to be the most efficient means of accomplishing action. It is, to those who still themselves long enough to notice, the supreme activity.

By focusing the mind on doing nothing, you are not making the mind quiet, you are entering the quiet that is already there, freeing yourself from mental gravity, floating to that oh-so-grand place where wonders wait to greet you. Buddhists call it practicing mindfulness. We call it practicing the present. No matter what tag you hang on it, when you relax the conscious hold over the subconscious, you open yourself to a universe of discovery—the vast cosmos of inexhaustible energies and boundless possibilities. While Western medicine insists that it is the brain that moves the body, the Zentrepreneur knows that it is the mind that moves the world. The ongoing trouble is that, since always, humans have tried to squeeze the mind into the brain, never realizing that it won't fit.

Know better.

Make way for insight. Clear a wide path. Thoughts are the ancestor to every idea. Turn off and tune in. Put up a sign: Do Not Disturb—Workin' on My Own Dream. Get purposeful. Get passionate about creating the results you desire. Dial in to the infinite radiance that is you. Recognize, please, that your creative inspiration, your dream, is waiting to honor you with audacious action. Penetrate into absorption, embrace your imaginative power, and do not resist letting in that which wants to be let in. Become, in the best sense, self-possessed. Make the opportunity to get to know what you want, what you feel. For all things have their inner truth, and to discover your own, you simply have to silence yourself to hear it calling.

Allow yourself sufficient time for stillness. Do not feel guilty about withdrawing or taking time out, for inaction is the most efficient means of accomplishing that there is. It is the oneness that comes when you are completely absorbed with full attention on what you are doing, so much so, that non-action is the action. In other words, the very basis of not doing requires quite a whole lot of doing. The Chinese sage Lao Tzu wrote that you must take action to attain non-action. Einstein, who was only smarter than all of us, said, "All meaningful and lasting change starts first in your imagination, then works its way out." Start from there. Imagination, not invention, is what transforms us. By making the effort to enter the inner, you dispense with time and enter the timeless, allowing innate aliveness, inspiration, a more active imagination to emerge unimpeded. It is this opening up to this great mergence that can awaken and transform you and set you on your path to empowerment.

Now we don't want to get all mystical about this, and we know that a lot of you are way too busy with the practical affairs of your day job to entertain thoughts about dealing with the hubbub of meditation, yoga, reiki, tai chi, aikido, or any of the number of reflective arts, but please believe that happiness is screaming for us, if only we would quiet ourselves long enough to listen.

Make the time to find the time to create the space for revelation. Relax into receptive stillness, allowing your mind to wander where it will. Research has shown that on average, our minds are busied with some 60,000 thoughts a day. Somehow or other, mute the chatter and clutter that occupies your noodle. If you want to discover and empower your dream you must be willing to take the concentrated action to quiet yourself. The quieter you go, the louder the voice of your heart will become. It is this wondrous voice, your intuition, that is the delicious fruit of solitude. It provides you with your most powerful innate resource, the all-so-great power to silence your doubts, your confusion, your fear of taking control of your own life, as well as the power to overcome the external resistance and frustrations that lie waiting for us all in the dark wood of reality.

Imagine that.

Exactly the point. Imagination is your power to go beyond the known and the unknown to create your utopia. Artist Paul Gaugin stated, "I shut my eyes in order to see." It's lamentable that our focus is always on what exists rather than on what could exist. To that we say, become an imagineer! Pay attention to your imagination, intuition, insight, and inspiration, the flashes that come from out of whatever divine blue, for this is the stuff that dreams are made of. Be alert and sensitive to the finite notes that strike a chord and rock you. Listen to it. Grab hold of it. Shake it and see what falls out.

Then, and this is paramount, quickly write it down before it shifts, alters, and goes thud, never to return. Francis Bacon advocated, "A man would do well to carry a pencil in his pocket, and write down the thoughts of the moment." Splendid advice, since the spark of one idea gives birth to another, which in turn creates another idea that can support, enhance, and empower actions that help materialize the idea into a reality. That's the magic of awareness. Ideas have a wonderful symmetry. You embrace an idea because you need an idea and because it needs you. With this very much in mind, keep a notebook handy at all times. Or a legal pad. Or a day planner. Or 3x5 cards. A microcassette, digital recorder, or text messager. If you have a handheld computer, good for you. I have one but found that the lunatic thing works me more than I can work it. Not important. What is important is that you provide a space for ideas to land when they come around circling.

Because an idea is a thing with feathers.

They can fly away as easily as they come, never to revisit you again. What enlivens and excites can be momentary and ephemeral, if it is not acted upon. Take this on faith, when God in all Her wisdom decides to provide you with creative unfoldment, do not let it get away. Get it down. Record it before it leaves you.

Aside: Rolling Stone and crypt kicker, rock god Keith Richards wrote the forever famous guitar riff for "Satisfaction" after waking up in the middle of the night in a hotel room. When he crawled out of bed the next afternoon, he had forgotten he'd written a song until he played his cassette recorder later that day and heard himself muttering the now rock-classic tune. End of aside.

Be a thinker-upper/writer-downer.

The point to be polished here is that even if you have an elephant's memory, by writing down your idea, and this is crucial, you create its existence in tangible form. You can see it, feel its charge of energy, and go back to it again later to review and consider if it still excites and fills you with positive feelings and purpose, because, in time, some ideas stiffen, while some remain such wonders the next time and the time after the next time.

Keep an idea log. Maybe it's a journal or whatever name you honor it with, do not deprive yourself of this vital instrument of manifestation. An idea log is a powerful tool to assist you in building the foundation and framework for empowering your dream. And if this seems like some off-the-wall suggestion, know that museums, universities, and private collections the world over, house the imaginative jottings of Archimedes, Michelangelo, da Vinci, Copernicus, Picasso, the Wright brothers, and Einstein, just to name hardly any. Truth to know is that there exists a lengthy written trail of providential bursts, cultivated revelations penned by the hand of their creative greats. Tangible reminders of ideas recorded to ensure that they didn't get lost in the tumult of daily events. No wonder that since 1978, the Smithsonian and Rutgers University have been hard at work archiving the over 5 million pages of ideas, notes, and other papers that Thomas Edison left behind. Fortunately for our hyper-inattentive world, Edison knew that a sharp mind deserves a sharp pencil.

So when you luck into an idea, write it down. That's the best basic advice for empowering your dream. Keeping an idea log is, at once, a very important way of knotting together action and reaction. A process for allowing connectives to click, which can bring into form ideas that can create energy, thoughts that can lead to actions, dreams that can turn into living realities. An idea log is, in sweet reality, a portfolio of possibilities. When geeky Billy Gates began to visualize the software that would change the daily revolving of the world, he made his mark, pressing pencil to paper, recording his bright efforts, delivering destiny. William Wordsworth said, "Fill your paper with the beating of your heart." Giving your idea a palpable presence is the very first step in looking at what wants to be looked at, transforming it from a flash of mental energy into a charge of physical energy. You will find it amazing, fascinating, reassuring, and absolutely faith-building when you begin to document and keep track of how many good ideas you have. Imagine the unimagined, ideas come from a new way of thinking.

And believing.

Okay if I flashback to another poem I've held onto all these years? It's by George Bernard Shaw and I'd like to take this moment and share it with you dear readers as an underscore.

"Some men see things as they are, and say, 'Why?'

I dream of things that never were, and say, 'Why not?'"

Learn to think differently and you will discover the different. Listening to what is truly inside yourself, allowing the sudden illumination of spirit, the whisperings of instinct to be captured and inked, is an invaluable practice that actually allows things to happen. The point to be made here is that by putting on paper your ideas you are programming yourself to accept the possibility of probability. And this is pivotal.

Another thing: There is no set-in-stone specification for blueprinting an idea log. It is a practice as unique as the individuals who undertake the task. Some carry their ideas in their log book, others create and deposit them in an idea bank—a file folder, binder, envelope, or computer database, a place where the ideas continue to grow interest by adding other gleaned information and support materials such as magazine articles, newspaper clippings, pictures, brochures, and trade journals. Develop a dossier. Tear stuff out. Attach. Thicken. Make more notes. Tinker. Zoom in. Elaborate. Expand. Expound. Stretch. Prune. Ponder. Go over your idea. Get under it. Begin to believe you can move a mountain. Believe you can move others. Know you can move yourself. No simple amusement, regard this exercise as a practice, designed to provide you with an accumulating knowledge and guidance that can create your dream future. A comparative dynamic of this can be seen mirrored in the element of water. Water can be one drop, or if gathered together, it can become a large sea, teeming with life.

Forever creating.

Realize that you are at all times sublime, each moment standing at the crossroads of what is and what can be. You may not want to hear this, but you should: It's all up to you.

The one simple truth is that it is you, repeat you, who must undertake the brave behavior that will empower your dream. You who must dare to take the dares. You who must be prepared to penetrate the process. We urge you to become a provocateur of potential. A deliverer of D-I-F-F-E-R-E-N-T. Dream big. Size matters. Dream wild. Boundlessness matters. Dream WOW. Wackiness matters most. Delight in the openness of possibilities. Then, consecrate your creative vision by dedicating to giving it shape and form. There's craft involved. Your destiny truly is in your own hands.

Closing in, we now live in an age of rapid technology, innovation, and change, where dollar notebooks have harbored million dollar ideas. Proving that the simple act of writing an idea is more than putting pen to paper, it is an assertive way of endowing yourself with ascendancy, helping you to become a more powerful creative thinker, providing you with the infusion of certain confidence and emotional energy necessary to importantly acquire the ability to approach your life with a mindful sense of discovery, creativity, and imagination. Most importantly, this restructuring the way you think will reshape the way you are, resulting in the unfolding of the inevitable, allowing only just the right idea to embrace you. Understand, an idea, even a possibility of a dazzler, can fan the flames of your dreams and desires. It will uplift and inspire, filling you with zest and zeal to achieve whatever you dare to dream possible. No matter what dark corner you choose to hide, the truth is this—once the idea has you in its power, at its mercy, it can do with you what it will. Then, the rest is up to someone else.

That someone, in case you still didn't know, is you.

Chapter Three
BECOME AN ACTION HERO

LIFTING WAITS

The true strength of a silent and still tiger

is its quickness to action.

Before we move on, we are going to ask a favor from you, followed by a quick question that Ron and I are comfortably convinced that no one with this book in their hands will answer correctly. First, so there is zero chance any of you will cry foul, we want you to know that Alexander Graham Bell filed a patent application at the United States Patent Office on February 14, 1876.

Now the favor: Read the following extracted patent-filing riff from that very day of February 14, 1876:

To all whom it may concern: Be it known that I have invented a new art of transmitting vocal sounds tele-graphically, under which a specification: It is the object of my invention to transmit the tones of the human voice through a telegraphic circuit, and reproduce them at the receiving end of the line, so that actual conversations can be carried on by persons at long distances apart.

Okay. On we go. The question we're going to now ask you is this: Who invented the telephone?

Hmmmm.

Knowing that none of you came up empty, quick to answer with the legendary Bell, let us be just as quick to tell you that you are only wrong!

The truth?

Going backwards, the above-captured filing was made by another involved in the world of invention named Elisha Gray, founder of the Western Electric Company and someone who had been granted patents on seventy other breakthrough discoveries. And what he had toiled so tirelessly on and finally accomplished was going to be such a terrific great thing that no one would believe it. But because he decided to run a few errands on that good and cold February day, it left Alexander Graham Bell to confidently pell-mell in and apply for a patent on his own apparatus only two hours ahead of Gray, shifting fame, fortune, and forever pasting Bell up there golden with the immortals.

Amazing.

Even more amazing is this, once the sludge was

stripped away, the genuine gasper was Bell's telephone didn't work. Gray's did!

But that didn't matter. None of the ensuing arguments mattered. In the end it didn't matter who you were rooting for in 1876, since the battle between the attorneys was merciless, the litigation taking years until the wizards on the Supreme Court ruled the stunner that, even though Bell's invention didn't work and Gray's did, the caveat crusher was Bell filed the idea first, and that, sadness of sadness for Gray, was that.

Now, this of course was madness, and you, me, we cannot imagine what it would have been like the rest of Gray's days. The blinding awfulness. The terrible torment. How horrible waking up deflated every morning of the world, a knife in your heart, the demons of remorse your constant companion, the unendurable tick-tocks of a clock always echoing in your ears to remind you of what might have been. Which brings us to a sacred samurai warrior maxim as good as any: When action speaks, words mean nothing.

Okay, fellow Zentrepreneurs, please remember this uncomplicated mantra of advice: NOW is the time for action—NOW is the place for action—NOW is the need for action.

Stop procrastinating.

Immediately!

Your future is created by how you live NOW!

The actions you take today will determine your tomorrows. In order for success to occur, you must create a sense of urgency to do—to act on the great idea for your life. To delay in taking direct, assertive action is to relinquish your well-deserved right to achieve your deepest desires. The past is made only of the past. The future is made only of the present. No matter what time of day you check your watch, the only time is now. Time behind is gone, the time ahead is unfixed. Now is the only place in time you have to outwit uncertainty. Living in the now is true living. The Zentrepreneur knows that time is hard to find and easy to lose. Learn to regard now as the great gift of opportunity—this is why it is called the present.

Confucius wrote, "The nature of people is the same—it is their habits that separate them." How true. Your success is not determined by luck, it's determined by the actions you choose to take each and every day. We know this.

And we believe this: The tragic drama that is connected to our concept of timing is that we tend to put off action, waiting for just the right time and just the right place to act, while the very act of waiting actually pushes desired events away from us. A self-inflicted analysis paralysis.

The Taoist master Guan Yin Tzu urged not to waste time calculating your chances for success or failures. Just fix your aim and begin.

Do not wait for things to happen to you. Go out and happen to things. Wishing, hoping, waiting for God to smile down will not create an environment where you will flourish. Regardless of your current situation, you must do something toward empowering your dream every day. You simply must accomplish an action. The fact that you chose to read this book is an action. Taking the time to think about who you are and what you really want out of life is an action. Even the simple act of committing yourself to want to do better is an action. Purely believe that every beginning is half of every action. As you embark upon an action toward the accomplishment of your goals, you are demonstrating to the world, but more importantly to yourself, that you are serious about attaining them. Once you come to understand that action transforms, you will realize that there is no difficulty in taking action, only effort.

So please do not just nod your head when you read this.

Please do not hesitate.

Please do not stand still.

And please do not think that the world will wait for you. Right now, the planet is slaloming though space at over 30,000 stellar miles an hour. You've got to become action oriented. Great things are happening below and above the surface. What we're trying to tell you is this: Embrace every opportunity to act, knowing that the universe reacts to action not to aspirations, desires, or hopes.

Wishing takes no effort but accomplishing demands purposeful, present action. Interestingly, the word *action* has within it the immediate directive to ACT-ON. You must act on your inspiration, your intuition, your vision, your purpose, and, above all else, your passion—that deepest well of your being that empowers you to have what you desire. No need for you to do any crystal-ball gazing. If you want to see into your future, simply look into your present actions. Noble Prize Laureate Thomas Mann advised, "Act like a man of thought, think like a man of action." How simple. Take deliberate, conscious control of transforming longing into definite performance. Realize always, please, your dream will not begin unless you do. Creating whatever you desire is only an action away.

Be an action hero.

This matters more than anything. Act on what interests and excites you. Obsessively. You don't have to do it full time, but you do need to make the time to take the time to do it. Prove to you inner core that you are serious about empowering your dream. To be a painter you must paint. To be a dancer you must dance. To be a craftsman you must create. To be a musician you must make music. If your dream is to open a business, then draw up a business plan—do not concern yourself with the needs and wants of start-up capital, but go through the motion of creating the plan anyway, re-alizing that you absolutely must continually take tangible actions toward attaining your dream. Rea-son. Transformation requires ongoing, channeled action. In order for your dream to manifest in the realm of reality, you must act a lot more than a lit-tle. Between heartbeats, the stalking tiger can go from slow fluidity to a powerful burst of energy, proof that the tiger knows that there is no path to action—that action is the path. You too are imbued with the magnificent tiger spirit of intuition and timing. You need only begin to dare.

The more you take action, the more confident you will become with your ability to take action. You must never, ever underestimate your capacity to empower your energies into a determined effort to realize the life of your dreams. Success is not determined by luck or prayer, it's determined by the actions you choose to take each and every day. To act on without hesitation or doubt will always awaken the greatness within. Above all else, realize, you must do to be. And please remember, while some search for something to do, a Zentrepreneur does what clearly needs to be done.

And the universe moves.

There is a touchstone in East Indian philosophy that states everything happens as it does because the universe is as it is. Meaning that it is through our actions, or lack of, that our destiny is shaped. Fasten yourself to the fact that the universe is a giving partner, waiting to rearrange itself according to our actions. That every action influences the future, action and reaction interlacing and building upon one another to create a new state of the universe until it is changed again by the next series of actions. The physics mavens tell us that the universe is not made of things—it is made of activity, events, and processes. Actions that react to actions taken by you. Goethe, the German philosopher, said, "The moment one definitely commits oneself, then Providence moves too." The universe merges and participates with dynamic patterns of action. However, as empowering as the cosmos is, it does not give us what we dream—it gives us what we take action on. A Zentrepreneur realizes that the secret to the magic life is to recognize that the way the universe works is the way we work—for the universe is us, always becoming itself, at the same time like us, changing into something else.

Prepping for destiny.

Briefly. There are many pure-pleasure perks that come as a result of authoring these Zentrepreneurial Guides, but way up there on the list is the enormous amount of correspondence that finds its way to us, and it finds its way to us from all over the world. And since we are not totally without ego, let me say we get inundated. E-mailers unending asking for guidance that can escort them through the winding maze of life. And yes, we do the best we can to answer each and every, sometimes getting the languages translated a bit of a bother, but everyone assumes, correctly, that we will somehow read them and hopefully in someway answer them, which we do. And if I had to nutshell it, the one single snippet expressed the most often by would-be Zentrepreneurs is, "I wish I knew what to do." To which we simply say, "Do something that needs to be done." Next case.

One of mine and Ron's wouldn't-it-be-great ideas is to convince Nike to reinvent their "Just Do It" slogan to "Just Did It." How marvelous to encounter such a proud proclamation displayed on T-shirts and caps by ordinary individuals who have become extraordinary doers, self-made action heroes who have crossed the great divide from the realm of ideas to the realm of action. To translate a dream into a reality takes more than intention, it takes becoming a master in making things happen. It takes desire, commitment, and purposeful action. And it takes it everyday.

We hope that it's clear to you by now that to answer the call to action doesn't require that you be bestowed with boots, cape, and super powers. The good news is that it takes nothing more than an awakening within. The bad news is that in order to empower your dream, like any action hero, you better be ready to battle a monster. And for those of you who are lunatic enough to believe that real

life monsters don't exist, guess what—a nightmare
of one lies waiting for you when you turn the
page ...

Chapter Four
FROM KNOW FEAR TO NO FEAR

CULTIVATE YOUR COURAGE

A tiger lives without fear,

with one glance it sees the truth.

No bad dream, the path to empowerment is a perilous one, horridly fraught with panic, terror, loneliness, risk, rejection, and failure, lurking beasties bad enough, but you better know now that none come at you more killingly cruel than the icy dread grip of fear.

Make no mistake, fear will reach out and snatch you from your wants and desires, hold you in its slavering grasp, prevent you from ecstatically living a life well lived. Fear skulks us in many a frightening form and even if you are bright and skilled, and courage has never been your enemy, fear can take over our good senses, permeating us with insecurity, anxiety, vagaries, and doubt. And you know the scariest thing?

We let it.

The truth is simply this—many, most, are shackled by fear. Weighed down with what Ron and I call the ponderous gravity of *atmosfear*—the fear of the unknown, the fear of failure, the fear of sacrifice, the fear of commitment, the fear of not having control, and believe it, even the fear of success. But there are reasons, good ones, why this occurs, and we will get to them in the pages ahead, but first know that most of the wise ones, the social scientists and psychologists, subscribe to the assessment that part of our brains are a reservoir for fear, which is why our noodles are hot-wired to release adrenaline, endorphins, and all sorts of hormones into our systems as a survival mechanism called the fight-or-flight response. Going back to the days when we first started coming down out of the trees this was an automatic trigger, a self-protective instinct, a surge of physical power given to alert us that our lives were in danger and to be prepared to summon up the appropriate response. If some saber-tooth tabby was coming your way, your self-protective instinct warned you that you needed to immediately take corrective action or be dragged into the bush and become a monster's munchie. This feeling of fear remains within us still today, which is why we think twice before stepping out in front of a barreling-down-the-street Buick.

What we want to impart to you here is that fear messages, which tell us our lives are in danger, are meant to be met with caution. But all the rest of our fears are meant to be met with courage. The fear of taking a risk, the fear of ridicule or that someone will disapprove of your goals and dreams, have everything to do with the survival of your self-image and nothing to do with the survival of your bodily being. These fears in large measure are the result of learning and conditioning, amplified by a lack of confidence and other suppressed feelings and mental torment, all obstacles that can keep you from your ultimate goals. There is an ancient Zen dictum that declares, "The obstacle is the path." Still so true. By adopting a different perspective, by bringing awareness and confronting certain realizations instead of avoiding them, you can release and liberate yourself from the thwarting clutches of anxiety, the enemy of empowerment and transformation. Easy to say, but you need to know that getting there is not a whole lot of fun. Because what you have to do is more than just only face your fears—no, much more traumatic than that, you have to face yourself and go on to identify what it is that's going on in your bean. Scary stuff sure, but do not be content to live your life in avoidance or denial of your fears. Understand that even enemies have enemies and the enemy of fear will always be your courage to conquer it. It's as simple and as complex as that.

Complex, indeed, because in order to discuss fear rationally you have to start with knowing that fear is not a rational thing. Fear is perception, a vapor, a sulfurous illusion, a pondering of possible "what ifs" our mind creates to silence the voice of the heart. The mind goes tripping, manufacturing "if you do" consequences, negative scenarios that can keep you from your promising future, glued forever, spending your days in blinding pre-dictability, settling for what might have been. Sad, sad, sad.

Emerson said, "Fear defeats more people than any other thing." We say, "Have no fear and trust your instincts." That's the important message we want to wallpaper you with here. Rise above the battle-taking place within you, letting it go on without you, realizing, that deep inside, your heart has the predominant power to guide you down your true path of purpose and success.

Quick time-out.

We'd like to pause here for a few secs to have you perform a physical exercise that we hope you will commit to memory. And for those of you who have just rolled your eyes, you will be thrilled to know that even though you will be required to flex a muscle or two, no heavy lifting is involved. To prove it, here we go. When we give the word, without thinking why or what for, will all of you, dear readers, please, just simply and quickly point with your finger to yourself. That's it. That's all. Ready?

Drum roll . . .

Set . . . Point!

Did any of you point to your head? We bet, with no doubt whatsoever, that none of you did, rather each and all of you instinctively pointed to your heart. And with good reason. The authentic you, the you that yearns to express and experience joy and bliss, the you that holds the power to live life and be what you are, the you that can overcome the blocking barriers of fear and empower your dream, resides in the haven of the heart, not in the conflicts and confusion of the mind. While the mind tries to tell us what will be, the heart holds out the wonder that can be. Alas, allowing us to reach the judgment that hope is more important than fear. You must not allow your fears to sabotage whatever dream you want to do or have. Always bear in mind, please, that how we choose to respond to the miscreant challenge of our fears is ultimately up to us. Only. Period.

For fear is an unreal response that holds whatever power we grant it. It is the perception of a result our mind puts forward as possible scenarios of the future that instills us with shakes of panic and frazzles us with fear. Making the invisible visible and giving it a face cause anxiety and create a dreadful anticipation for whatever bleak consequences we imagine may lie ahead. The key word that just went by is imagine. The feeling of fear is nothing more than a fantasy, a response that we create to deal with the pondering of the unknown. It is not the supposed result that is frightening, but the anticipation of it that becomes so scarifying. We are fearful not so much by what will happen, rather we are fearful of what it is that might happen, dwelling on the possible consequences of certain outcomes. To shoulder the comprehension that the feeling of fear is more powerful than the actual thing we fear itself is to begin to untangle yourself with hope. Getting up to speak in front of a group— very overwhelming for some, but when done, survival rules the day. Same happens with those who break into the sweats when a test looms large or their airplane takes off. When all is said and done, you won't need a mirror to see that you're still standing. The point that needs to again be mentioned here is that most of our fears are actually unfounded—they are not real, they are phantasms of our own making that only exist because we allow it.

Listen, at one time or another we will all have a monster under the bed. Fear is as much a part of the mix of empowering your dream as the dream itself. Fear is inevitable, its part of the baggage we all bring along the dream-seeking trail. Accept that fear can be defeating or defeated, a natural piece of the process. Once you accept this, you gain the empowerment to master it. And to help you do just that, please take the time to tattoo the following acronym behind your eyelids. The core of it will go a long way in helping you zero in and zero out your fears:

F.E.A.R.
Face it.
Engage it.
Assess it.
Reject it.

Remember how we said some fears are based on real danger and some are not? The dictionary throws this bunch of words at us defining fear: anxiety caused by the anticipation of real or imaginable danger. In other words, fear—true fear—is a reaction that alerts you to an actual, immediate danger signal that is happening in the now, kicking your gears into an instantaneous fight-or-flight mode. Other fears are the ones that we allow to invade and dominate our minds, the result of an anticipation of a future unknown—that something bad could happen, but there is no real danger that is actually happening now. The picture should be coming clear; it is this fear of anticipating the unknown, a denial or avoidance of a possible outcome that is one of the all-too-common reasons why many hold the magnificence of their lives hostage, suffering for their sins.

Don't try to solve it. Dissolve it.

Learn to dispel your fears. Realize that fear is nothing more than an ominous black cloud you choose to stand under, a feeling of gathering dread that you allow to blot out the wonder and light of your potential horizon. Now we don't know a whole lot of things, but what we do know is this:

With open-minded willingness, sometimes there's a rainbow so quickly.

Face your fear.

Take a moment to recognize the fear for what it is. Ask yourself is this a real fear—is the danger you feel real? Assuming that you are not putting yourself in any physical harm's way, and you're going to make it out alive, ask yourself what it is that you are most afraid of? More than likely, if you muster the courage to be honest enough to question the veracity and validity of your fear, you will only 110 percent of the time come to the conclusion that you are the willing victim of an insanely melodramatic scenario of your own imagination. Marcus Aurelius said, "Look things in the face and know them for what they are." Facing your fear means that you are ready to face many truths, the most important truth being that you must get to know the knower. Fears are an invitation for you to identify certain characteristics of your life that either make you feel eager to move forward or make you afraid to act. Ask yourself the questions: What is it that you are fearful of? Is it the the fear of change? Is it the fear of rejection? Is it the fear of insecurity? Is it the fear of losing control or respect? Is it the fear of failure? These are not fears of self-preservation—these are fears of self-protection of ego only, an arrogance that sabotages your success. Facing your fear squarely without denying or repressing it, or allowing yourself to be a victim of it, can be very tricky on the psyche, but doing so gives you the power to distinguish between rational fear and irrational fear. The transcendental truth is that if you hold what you fear up to the light, the reality of it will begin to fade, allowing you to re-take control of your thinking process and your destiny. The best thing.

Engage your fear.
Use your fear instead of allowing it to use you. Life would be just so much a happier place if you would recognize your inborn courage to step outside your comfort zone and engage your fears by confronting them. Staying home and dry, within the confines of a safe life, not empowering yourself to step beyond what you know isn't too difficult, risking little, is a passive choice because you are aware of your fears. But being aware means nothing—what you need to do is get to know them. Make a friend of your fear. Visit with it. Interview it

objectively, as an interested observer rather than a participator. This way you can separate your thoughts from your feelings, creating an emotional distance that allows you to understand the reasons for your fear, whatever its shape, thereby getting out from under its control. The whiz behaviorists believe that most fears are nothing more than learned coping patterns and, like other personal proclivities, can be unlearned by trusting your true self and doing what you need to do. Instead of dwelling on your self-doubts, picturing the menace that waits, visualize your dream, focus on the specific image of the desire you seek. Passionately believe in the probability of succeeding in turning your dream into a reality. Passion empowers. The more passionate you are about living your dream, the more you will begin to assert control over your fear. And while you may never rid yourself of having fear as a constant companion, you can learn to take charge of your teeth clenching, and decide how much you will allow your fear to be a part of your life, how much of an influence you will allow it to have on the kind of life you wish to have. The sage one knows that it is not the inner fears that matter, it is how we live with their presence that counts the most. Once you have chosen to engage your fear, you will quickly come to discover that the only future fear has is the one you choose to allow it. Amen to that.

Assess your fear.

A not-so-terrible task when you come to accept that fear is ultimately rooted in perception, not in reality. A Zen master tells the tale of a man who was afraid of his shadow. He ran faster and faster then he ever ran before to get away from it, but the faster he ran, the more he tired while the shadow did not. He ran for as long and as hard as he could, until finally he ran himself to death. Now whether you agree that this is a wonderful little story or not, when somebody wise gives you the benefit of wisdom, you would do well to listen. In other significant words, stand still when fear assails you. Assess the feelings that have come to haunt you. Gain awareness of your true reality by refusing to allow yourself to become a breeding ground for panic. Dispel the demons. Be truthful and honest with yourself, and ask what is the absolute worst possible thing that can happen to you if you choose to ignore your fear? The questions that should be asked, must be asked, are what are the consequences—is it discouragement, temporary discomfort, possible ridicule, the loss of someone else's approval? Take this on faith, these things, no biggie. A Zentrepreneur must be willing to risk the negative in order to accomplish the positive. By candidly assessing the consequences, please know that the fear becomes weaker and you become stronger. As you experience this genuine inner transformation and change, you will gain courage and become excited to leave the safety of the known for the opportunities awaiting you in the unknown. Logically assessing your fear and reappraising the reasons you allow its hold can go a long way to unstoppable confidence, releasing fear's horrific hold on you. Which is, after all, what you want, when a monster haunts your dreams.

Reject your fear.
Arm yourself with attitude, knowing that you have the inborn power to create your own reality. Instead of allowing yourself to be a victim of fear, be a victor over fear by affirming your tiger heart and tiger mind, your deep inherent courage to face challenge and overcome any obstacle. Remember always, it's up to you to claim your dream. You're the one who has control over your own thoughts, feelings, and actions. Take responsibility for the

power that you have to reject uncertainty and go after the fullest potential of your life. Fear and anxiety weaken. Hope and courage strengthen. Squelch the intimidation of fear, exert your will to transform, to change, to conquer any adversities and doubts. Know that most of your fears are unfounded. Failure, rejection, ridicule, the disapproval from others, these are fears that others have packed into your bags for the great journey ahead. Finding these things too heavy a burden, many abandon the quest. Do not let fear be your undoing. When the flames start to flicker and the wolves begin to howl, know that you are in control of your life. Aspire with passion, perseverance, intensity, and, above all else, courage. Courage is not the absence of fear—it is acting in spite of fear.

Shaping the point, we go with the one time salvation of Western civilization, Winston Churchill, who viewed courage as the place to start, saying, "Courage is the first of human qualities, because it is the quality which allows all the others." Only too true. It's important to know that there are hundreds of helps out there, a world of books, techniques and tapes, wonderful stuff that you can seek to master your fears. And if any of it offers a list of steps to take to overcome the suffocating crush of fear, don't even bother to go on to step two if the first step is not courage. Now is as good a time as any to tell you that you will never, ever, no matter what, live your dream if you don't have a lot of that. Prayers alone mean nothing. It takes more than looking to the heavens. In order to live a life divine, it simply comes down to having the courage to do so....

It always does.

Chapter Five
WALK THE TALK

DETERMINE YOUR
DIRECTION

To all who seek the truth,

a tiger walks like a tiger.

In the interest of accuracy, here is an absolute certainty: The path to empower your dream requires you to go from good to better, from better to best. This is true for all of us. Has to be. Because in order to manifest the success you seek, you have to wield the will to transform, improve, and evolve, continually embracing new ways of doing and being. Unless you are prepared to overcome the inertia of complacency and its mesmerizing effects of *c'est la vie*, you will attain little, languishing in the realm of what is easily available rather then achieving the greatness that awaits.

You must act your way into a new way of thinking. Interestingly, a keystone of Buddhist philosophy comes to mind: "We are what we think." It's an unspoken sadness that many repeat the same thoughts and behaviors over and over again, hoping for a different result. Recognize that each moment need not be a repeat of the past, but instead can be and is a moment of a new beginning. A moment of serendipitous opportunity to empower yourself with the positive force of clear, life-affirming thoughts. Do not live your life the way you have been living it if you want new results. The Zentrepreneur knows that if what you are doing is not creating the change you wish to see, then change what you're doing.

One of the foundations to sustained personal success is understanding that to take control of our destiny, we must take control of our thoughts. How and what we think will determine our future. When it comes to living your dream, whether you think you will or you won't—you're right.

Act as if you will.

Act as if you are serious about attaining your dream. Walk, talk, and act enthusiastically creating a single-minded attitude of success toward the results you desire. The warrior knew that it was not his sword that struck. Striking the opponent was achieved through a state of mind and attitude. Armed with the ultimate weapon of concentrated confidence, the warrior wielded a total presence. Adopt this warrior mindset. The attitude you hold about yourself decides your destiny. You are not as you think you are, but as you think. Positive thoughts uplift and produce positive results. Negative thoughts produce negative results that cripple and, worse, crush your emotional core. One of America's pioneering psychologists, William James, said that the greatest discovery is that man can alter his life simply by altering his attitude of mind. We'll spare you the quotes and tell you that what he advocated was that if you act as if you are what you want to be, then you will become that. This "act as if" principle is a powerful method of converting your consciousness from conditioned habits into specific positive behaviors that will not allow you to be defeated by your own self-destructing, negative feelings. Now not wanting to put our ignorance on display, let us say that we know nothing about psychological babble, but we do know this: By deciding to take control of your inner thoughts and attitudes, by engaging positive convictions and emotions, you go out into the world traveling the glorious path of will, a remarkable odyssey where positive attitude cultivates positive action, delivering you to that oh-so-special place where your dreams are waiting to have you.

Unless you say something that pushes them away.

Because words can do that. You need to be alerted to that fact that your words, your inner chatter absolutely can uplift or diminish. One of the great schisms of empowering your dream is that your words influence your beliefs, your beliefs influence your behaviors, and your behaviors influence the results that orbit your life. Here's the wisdom. Research has determined that we are constantly talking with ourselves, even though we are not conscious of this running internal dialogue that fills our head. This steady stream of self-speak is our ongoing encounter with the things we see, hear, and experience, stimuli that is translated into words that become patterns of conditioning and thought. This self-speak can be positive and empowering, or negative and defeating. Either way, it is what generates our emotions and activates our behaviors.

Words are not just words. They are inner directives flowing just under our surface of awareness. Your ongoing mission is to become aware of your self-speak so you can recognize and rechannel the stream that is running your feelings and behaviors. The ancient text of the *I Ching* uses the imagery of Wind over Water, which suggests that the rippling waves reflect all the moods of the skies. Watch your words, for it is your self-speak that creates your experience and helps you crest.

You must be master of your mind rather than be mastered by your mind.

A Zentrepreneur practices a consciousness of confidence. Empowering a dream is as personal as it gets. Create a cranium full of positive, upbeat self-assuredness. The quality of your life is ultimately determined by the quality of your thoughts. Pay attention to how often you are thinking about what you want versus what you don't want in your life. Be awake, diligent, and attentive to your self-speak. Behaviorists have found that eight out of every ten thoughts are negative. This 80 percent finding supports the dictionary's postings of two and half more negative words than positive words. So how do you go about standing vigilant at your mind's gate? For the simple solution, we need only look to the complicated computer world, which has the word GIGO that explains it all—Garbage In-Garbage Out.

Your internal dialogue is the downloaded software that has more to do with you catching and living your dream than any other determinant. Your thoughts create the entire direction of your life. You must take care to transform your negative thoughts into supportive self-speak, by catching it, identifying it, challenging it, and changing it. When you hear yourself manufacturing a negating mindset, you *must must must* halt it immediately. Inwardly verbalize the command "STOP" to yourself and change the sabotaging statements into direct empowering ones. For example, the words "I am" create one of the most positive statements the mind will agree with. Be cautious about the words that follow, treating them with care, for they reinforce habits that determine behavior and directly influence and guide your being. Do not attach "I am" with any negative thoughts. When you use statements such as, "I am not able to do this," the mind will accept this belief and shut down in agreement with the hopelessness you feel about yourself, resulting in an intellectual conundrum, preventing your inborn talents and gifts from coming to the rescue. If you say you can't do something, it is you who becomes the dark creator of the can't. If you say you will try, then you will only try. If you say that you hope, alas, you will dismiss your dream as a mere wish. Ahhh, but if you will say you will do something, then you initiate the commitment that begins the empowering-dream mating dance.

Doubt the doubt.

Do away with it.

When you master self-belief, your words become a source of strength with the power to manifest themselves. This cannot be stated enough or too strongly; it is your own words that can diffuse or empower your success. The Japanese have a saying, "One kind word can warm three winter months." Speak kindly to yourself. For if you, as a Zentrepreneur, aspire to live a dream, you must rid yourself from the tutorial tyranny of negative self-speak by consciously replacing it with the abundant potential of positive self-speak.

Okay, get ready now. Here comes a sample list of words that when bandied about will help carry the day. This list is just for us, so pay close attention.

Sabotaging words	Empowering words
I can't	I won't
I will try	I will do
If I	When I
I should	I could
I hope	I will
If only	Next time
This is a problem	This is an opportunity
I don't know	I will find out
I failed	I stumbled
I made a mistake	This is a learning experience
I'm frightened	I'm challenged
Life's a struggle	Life's an adventure

This small selective list is simply presented to illumine the point that conscious, carefully worded, positive statements are the rock of behaviors that help you shape your beliefs and realize your dream.

Through the use of empowering words, you empower yourself. Words form the thread of statements that weave our actions. Like a Zen garden, where the careful attention given to the placement of each object speaks to us, the same careful attention to our self-speak empowers our sense and spirit, providing mind-opening power allowing all of us to partake of infinity. What we say to ourselves has more of an impact than what others say about us. Quoting Hamlet in Shakespeare's great play about the human mind, "Words, words, words." Indeed. Gandhi said, "Keep your thoughts positive, because your thoughts become your words. Keep your words positive, because your words become your behavior. Keep your behavior positive, because your behavior becomes your habits. Keep your habits positive, because your habits become your destiny." The one simple fact that you must never forget is that the will and the willingness come from within. Every repeated act of resolve adds and strengthens. Through reinforcing and repetition, thread entwined becomes string; string entwined becomes rope; rope entwined, a cable. Success manifests from the inside out. What you tell yourself strongly effects your thoughts. Your thoughts determine what you do. What you do repeatedly will determine your results.

Your words are a potent transformative power. Speak to yourself in a confident, resolute way that demonstrates to your mind that you know the results you seek are going to happen. When your mind hears you talking with positive expectancy, it interprets, analyzes, and concludes that it must do everything it can to ensure your success. Words form belief, belief forms action. The words you use can make all the difference between being heartened and heart-broken. Pay attention to your self-speak with ongoing mindfulness. Your ability to choose a positive attitude is your most important resource for happiness. Make a choice and give it a voice.

Amazingly, once you learn to choose your words carefully, your life will never be quite the same again.

Chapter Six
SMART EFFORT, WORKING WISDOM

LOVE LEARNING

A tiger on the prowl knows all it needs.

For a fortunate few, it just seems to work out.

For the rest of us, empowering a dream takes a dedicated desire, an exertion of will, a consistent clinging to confidence, and yes, as a matter of course do you ever need courage, and undeniably, you have to persevere in the face of difficulties and doubts. But riding above it all is your commitment to the process of acquiring the knowledge and skills necessary to make your dream manifest itself, which is why it is crucial for a Zentrepreneur to remember this:

Learning is a moment that never ends.

To repeat, true Zentrepreneurs realize that no matter how great their knowledge, there is no end to learning, that each piece of knowledge leads to the next. As Zentrepreneurs, understand that the rock bottom of every success is the size of the chasm between the dream and the ability to bring it into being. The ancients were quick to advise that if you know that you don't know everything, then you know everything you need to know. The mind of a Zentrepreneur is like the ocean. All the rains and rivers can run into it without ever filling it up. Failure to catch and live your dream is simply a failure to know what you need to know.

Success is not man made. It's mind made. You must have the power of savvy, always learning and growing, with knowledge working for you. Subscribe to an ongoing process of self-expansion and discovery. Embrace an eagerness for continuous personal growth. Wisdom, not capital, is the quintessential currency needed to champion your idea. You must be open to the clean, clear reality that the pinnacle of wisdom is never done and never won. You will never know enough.

Stepping back, quick riff of a story.

After many years of training in the sword-smith's art, the student announced he had reached an advanced state of enlightenment and traveled to the high mountain to seek a position with a renowned weapon-maker for the samurai. Excited to show the breadth of his knowledge and skill, the student let the master swordsmith know that he was ready to begin making the greatest swords ever that day, assuring the master that his knowledge and training were complete. Days turned into weeks, and despite the many orders placed by the emperor to make weapons for his warriors, the master swordsmith never entered his forge. Until the first moonless night. In the total darkness, the wise and patient swordsmith set to work. Awakened by the heavy-hammer pounding of metal on the anvil, the student quick rushed to the forge to see the master swordsmith laboring in earnest. After the master swordsmith plunged the blade, edge down, into water, the student asked him why he had waited this very night to begin. The master was quick to answer, "Only during a moonless night can the color of the right temperature of the heated blade be seen." Amazed by the master's wisdom, the student asked, "How is it that you know such a thing?" To which the master swordsmith replied, "How is it that you do not."

There is a lesson here. More to the point, two lessons to be gleaned from this story as we travel the true path of possibility. First, when it comes to empowering our dream, we need to remember that we can never know all that there is to know. And the second, we all need to remember this, each and every step of the way.

Acknowledge knowledge. Please. Embrace an eagerness for continuous growth by dedicating your days to the ongoing quest to become your best. Equip yourself with attitudes, attributes, and skills that will turn you into a connoisseur of capability. Every dream requires you to gain knowledges that will help you improve, evolve, and excel. The barrier between you and your everlasting success will always be what, who, or the things you don't know. So for now and forever forward, get out there and learn what you don't know. Become more knowing tomorrow than you are today. Enroll yourself into a true course of miracles, take advantage of the free admission at what Ron and I want to tell you is the most important institution of higher learning that exists: EDUCATION U. (YOU). Cultivate your cranium. Build mental muscle. Rearrange the molecules of your mind with expansive erudition. Make it your daily mantra to maximize your mentality. A lesson learned is not an end, it is a means. Knowing something is not an accomplishment, it's a means of accomplishing. Choose to add to your learning because success only comes to people who grasp it, and wisdom is the all-important thing that e-x-t-e-n-d-s your reach. Do all this and more, but most importantly what you must do is this:

Admit your ignorance.

There. The secret's out. Truth to tell, it's difficult to learn anything if you think you already know it all. Let go and confess your lack of learnings. It is this letting go of this imperfection that becomes the beginning essence of your ultimate perfection. At the Republic of Tea we know that a great thing done is never perfect, but that doesn't mean it fails. Even in a perfect cup, there exists a hollow. It is this emptiness within it that makes it perfect. Without it, how would the tea leaves take the water? How would we drink the tea? To attain knowledge and wisdom we must remain open and empty, allowing ideas and insights, the tea of wisdom to pour in. To be empty, to admit how little we truly know, is to realize real abundance, to overflow with lessons learned. But in order to overflow, we must first be open to receive.

Admit your ignorance, and wisdom is waiting. Accept yourself for not knowing, and you simplify the journey. Einstein said, "The important thing is not to stop questioning." And hats off to that. Knowledge is what allows life to live us. When we are children, our thirst for knowledge is never masked, as we openly admit our ignorance, not afraid of peppering the air with the constant, repetitious queries of what and why. Our drive to learn is an all-consuming, exhilarated one, persisting with questions again and again until we receive satisfying answers filling us with WOW and wonder. It's unfortunate that as we become adults, we fear appearing unknowledgeable to others, so rather than opening ourselves up to learning something new, we close ourselves down, not wishing to look ignorant of certain facts, shutting off the opportunity of being the recipient of the great gift of learning. To accept thinking what we've been told to think is not thinking at all. Again, because it can't be repeated too often, it is the questions we ask or fail to ask that shapes our universe. It really saddens us that generation after generation are spoon-fed the appalling maxim, "What you don't know, can't hurt you." Well, it can. Tragically. Painfully. Even to utter such nonsense is the first nail in the coffin of a life unlived.

Be at all times ready to venture into the unknown. Only when we dare to unashamedly admit to our inevitable shortcomings will we enable true learning and empowerment to occur. Once we acknowledge that we don't know, we can do everything about it.

For the first time on planet Earth, our dreams need no longer be our fantasies. All of us, are living in an age where we are blessed beyond belief. No generation of human beings has ever had such vast resources of readily and easily accessible information to guide and direct. Recognize that the next best thing to having knowledge is knowing where and how to find it. Take the responsibility to achieve a vibrant state of mind. Perpetrate possibility through lifelong learning and growth. Organize and prioritize the knowledges and skills you require to empower your dreams and go after them with valiance and vigor. Seek out and take advantage of the years of other people's hard-won experience and expertise—their mistakes and their solutions can provide you with invaluable salvation. Read biographies of great individuals. Study success principles. Learn and develop techniques that will help you to overcome, such as speed reading, public speaking, writing, critical thinking, and leadership principles. Delve deeply. Dig in. Dig out. Discover renewal. Build a better brain. With apologies to the Ivy League halls, learning is not a science, it is an art. It is an ongoing practice. Practice which will not make you perfect, but it will make you better prepared to live your dream. Recognize that life is a continuing education course. So practice. Do a little, or do a lot. But become practiced in the art of learning. Just as Olympic athletes practice their sport, Zentrepreneurs practice their learning. Practice. Practice. Practice.

How magnificent that we live in an era where lifetimes of accumulated wisdoms, wellsprings of insights and inspirations are available to us instantly through the wild wired world of the Internet, or by spending moments with books, audiotapes, newspapers, magazines, articles, interviews, seminars, classes, CD-ROMs, all mediums from which you can learn many things, especially about yourself. Exert the will to transform, to improve to evolve. Be open to knowledge, live your passion, hone your strengths and skills, develop your talents, learn to set goals, find a mentor, choose to be happy, do all the things that we've covered in our other Zentrepreneur's Guides (which of course, you've read), knowing that unless you know what you know and know what you don't know, your dream will never happen. . . .

No matter how hard you try.

Chapter Seven

SURROUND SOUND,
THE VOW OF WOW

FIND SUPPORTIVE
SOMEONES

If you choose to ride the tiger,

you must go where the tiger goes.

Dear fellow dream dwellers ... There will be consequences.

There always is when you go after what you want. Because the process of transition from dream to reality is an arduous one. Your mind will see to that. The greater your goal, the greater you better be prepared to meet your new live-in roommates, the terrible tenants of difficulty, defeat, disappointment, and discouragement. A bruising bunch that will run rampant through your house of dreams, trashing your foundation of faith, punching holes in your passion and purpose, trying their destructive best to scuttle whatever it is that made you take the wonderful leap of faith to claim what you want and commit to what it takes to get it. More than any external barrier, it is this tremendous psychological power of drubbing yourself that causes you to feel overwhelmed, losing the will for what you desire or wish to be. Surrendering to the curse of inaction, balefully giving in to the difficult and discouraging, you become vulnerable to self-pity, the compulsion to look to someone outside yourself to deliver your dream. And don't you do it.

Mustn't happen.

Won't happen.

One of life's basic truths that needs to be stressed is that you are the only one who is responsible for your future. By which we mean, that if you sincerely think the people you know and like are looking at their watches waiting to put the spring back in your step, or chomping at the bit to deliver you a rainbow, don't fret. Just dig around for your receipt and take this book back just as fast as you can for a refund. No help here for dewey-eyed dreamers who count on the kindness of others or Divine grace.

Your truth is this: All is possible if you will only make a courageous commitment to rely upon yourself. No one else can journey the path for you. It is you who must walk in expectancy, counting only on yourself to be the relentless architect of your destiny. To live a dream is not a thing to be waited for, it is a thing to be achieved. More about that in the pages ahead. But, for now, know that Buddha said, "Wise men fashion themselves." We say, "Others may change the way you live, but only you can change your life." In order to achieve and succeed, you must wake up every morning of the world and be the rock of belief that drives you. Which is why it's crucial for you at the beginning, to become more than anything else . . . shhhh . . . a secret keeper.

At the start, when it comes to discussing your dream, tell no one. Not even a clue. Keep your dreams, your goals, and your plans to yourself. Because once you tell them of your heartfelt desire to do and to be, they will look at you strangely. Unfortunately many, maybe most, well-meaning friends and family members have issues of their own, which prevent them from offering a proper support structure. They may think of you in terms of a past experience and not of the person you can capably become. They will carefully say such crushingly killing things as:

—It's a stupid idea.

—It can't be done.

—You don't have what it takes.

—You're too old.

—You're too young.

—No way are you going to make it.

—Don't take the chance.

Your reaching out for assurance and self-grandeur at this so critical time will be met with statements that will pull you from your purpose and squash your spirit. Not stopping there, your passion and excitement will shockingly be challenged, putting you on the defensive, and what's so painful and tragically tough about that is that you will become distracted by their lack of approval or acceptance. So much so that their quick-minded dismissal of your plans and dreams will deeply etch away at your attention and focus. Putting up with who's putting you down, you will lash back to champion your confidence. Letting loose your ego, you will plunge into their cynicism. Trying to defend and explain, you'll be contributing to your own downfall by way of the dread degeneration of substituting talk for action. The undoing of us all.

So, shhhh ... Never a whisper.

No matter how exciting your expectations, or how your idea, product, service, or dream is so much a dazzler that you simply cannot contain your enthusiasm, you must understand the importance of taking Ron and Stuart's soul-sheltering Vow of WOW, a two-part promise of purpose that will only go a long way in helping you avoid gratuitous confrontation and heartbreak.

Regardless of how certain you are that others will be fully supportive of you, in the beginning, at the start, it's best to keep quiet about your plans. No chitchat about where your dream-heart lies. Alas, for reasons that pass understanding, we live in a world where only positive people are more likely to support positive people. Just as birds of a feather flock together, people of confidence cluster. Only people of goodwill who have positive attitudes about themselves can help you believe and achieve. People who don't won't.

Do not allow someone else's mingling of low self-esteem and self-doubt become your reality. Their negativity is their problem, don't let them make it yours. Distance yourself from those high-jackers of hope, who discourage, distract, drain, undermine, or would misguide—the world will etch away on them soon enough. Do not let them pull you from your purpose and clutter your confidence. Let them live their days darkened with shadow while you travel a life of sunny landscapes. Thoreau said, "The faultfinder will find faults even in paradise." No casual commitment, the Vow of WOW is your personal pledge to protect your dream from the skepticism and resistance of others.

Now we're not suggesting that you stay home with your shades drawn down and closed—what we do want to make clear is that you don't give others the power to pillage your passion. By having the autonomy to stay focused and attentive, you help yourself to help yourself. And then, when you are amazingly lucky (and never forget that you are), and you are full speed into the process of accomplishing your goals, that's the time to reveal what you want to do, with whom you want to, remembering repeatedly. ...

You are in charge!

You who get to choose who shares in the manifestation of your dreams. This, please note, is the second part of the Vow of WOW pact, the all-too-important, momentum process.

Once you have some of your accomplishments comfortably inside you, things going good, that's the time to let fly all your palpable energy to totally WOW those whose assistance and guidance are vital to empowering your dream.

Become the brilliant flame that draws people to the source. As a Zentrepreneur, those that you come in contact with will clearly be interested in who you are and what it is you want to do. Your Vow of WOW, your consciousness of confidence, your commitment to your true self, to your dream, will excite and ignite the spark in others, by exhibiting to one and all, through example, that you have chosen to fan the flames of your heart with your soul.

Elevate your thoughts and attitude to the highest level possible. Don't just catch lightning in a bottle—Can it! With all of the passion that you can, do and be the very best that you can, in every way that you can! When you go out there, and forever after, show that you are a person of fervor and exuberance that can carry the day. That you are someone who has a WOWerful will to live the life you love and that you are going to love the life you live. Learn to become a possibility thinker. Thinking possibility, believing in possibility, and pushing for possibility will draw the attention of other visionary people.

Very important.

Because for you to be at your best, you need a supportive someone. We all, always, need a supportive someone. So as a practical matter, dedicate yourself to engaging the kind of like-minded, positive people who can offer you knowledge and advice. The emotional reason is at least as important, for the right individuals can also provide you with the kind of understanding, nurturing, encouragement, and inner strength that can help inspire and guide you through promise and peril, making serendipity happen.

Form an action faction. Create a passion posse. Wrangle up other WOW warriors, peers who are equally possessed and share the same spine and spirit, and can assist you with the many battles you must face on your way to winning the war of accomplishment. Be with those who will help you be. People who have dreams of their own are more likely to support you in achieving yours. Notice the immediate spontaneous harmony when you surround yourself with those who exhibit the same passion for possibility and constancy of purpose that matches your own. Pay attention to how you feed off their energy, enthusiasm, reassurance, wisdom, and insights.

The *Tao Te Ching* teaches us that people who argue do not understand. And people who understand do not argue. As a very strong rule, keep the company of those who will listen, encourage, facilitate, and help enable you to stay on your path of personal growth and intention. Intention transforms reality. Stanislavsky taught that it doesn't matter whether you play well or badly, what matters most is that you play truly. The advice is as old as the world: By staying true to your intention, you will become the change you wish to see.

On a planet populated with dream-killers, you must shelter yourself with the help of dream-livers, those kindred spirits who will support you in your desire to grow and assist in keeping your dreams from getting ground in the dust. The common thread that weaves through people who have achieved any measure of success is that they have had the inspiration, help, and input of supportive others. As by way of a cultural example, we're sure there are many of you who park yourselves in front of the tube to watch the seemingly endless mélange of awful award shows. No harm. A sinful admission: At times, we do it, too. That out of the way, remember how you are invariably at the mercy of the winners who at their big moment use their acceptance speeches to tick off a very long list of thank-yous to those whose help had been for them a deliverance? Now there's a reason why they always, always make a point of doing this, and here it is:

They didn't get there on their own.

They don't just think this. They know it. In their dark nights, away from the adulation and the entourage, when their head hits the pillow and they're staring up at the ceiling in sleepless over-drive, in the corner of their heart that is still gen-uine, they keep the knowing of all the help that they received to get them to become darlings of the day. The true ones do. And yes, they have the fame, and of course the hyped look is in place, some even have talent, but for each and every that has been graced with success, they know that they didn't get there on their own. No one does. Which is why we want you forever forward to remember the follow-ing: When it comes to empowering our dreams, more than anything else, we all need all the help we can get, and we all need it, every step of the way.

The point to all this is simply to emphasize, and emphasize again, how important it is for you to surround yourself with the genuine head nodding of supportive someones, those miracle-makers who also live in a world where persistence overcomes resistance. Stay away from those who say they are behind you all the way. Get with those who will stand next to you and help you face the fire. Do everything you can to attach yourself to nurturing, affirming people who have a positive mind and provide a positive push, who in good times and bad, believe in your talents, passions, and dreams, having no doubt that you will one day WOWify the world with your accomplishments. Treat them with kindness unending for their advice and solace as you undertake the vow. Because as you journey through your years, they will be the anchors that will make a glorious difference in your life.

And when you sneak back into your memories and think about them, all those that kept you in their thoughts yesterday and the yesterdays before that, do us one, oh-so-small favor. . . .

Smile.

Chapter Eight
MAY THE FORCE BE WITH YOU

COMMITMENT

Within the frozen fix of a tiger lies its true strength.

It's an inside job.

In order to empower your dream, wanting to will not be enough. Intending to will not be enough. Willing to will not be enough. Wishing to will never be enough. To live a love-what-you-do, do-what-you-love-life takes more than high hopes. What you have to know is that to live your dream, you have to wake up and absolutely work for it. Endlessly. And that, fellow Zentrepreneurs, takes a confidence of conviction that there exists a no more powerful commitment than the one you make with yourself.

It is you and you alone who must undertake the ultimate responsibility for believing in who you are and what you are capable of. We've said it before, but thought you ought to be reminded: Do not expect others to bring forth your happiness and success. The Zen master Dogen once said, "I am not other people and other people are not me." When you resolve to accept that it is you who has the power to deliver your dream, you stop demanding or hoping that others will bestow on you or fulfill for you what you can only bestow on or fulfill for yourself. It is you who wields the power of choice for your life. Your truth is that you are the one who gets to choose between a life of chance or a life of choice. When it comes to what differentiates those who do and those who don't, commitment is the single most important factor.

While motivation is the result of some external source—someone or something that encourages you to take action, commitment is an internal force. It differs from motivation in that no one can make you committed. You may do what others ask of you for many a reason, but are you doing it because you are specially committed? Only you can provide the answer. Commitment happens internally. Again:

It's an inside job.

Commitment is a resplendent swirl of energy, comprised of your desire, values, and beliefs, the all-consuming zeal that originates from your internal radix, the spirit that nurtures the greatness of your soul, the belief that drives you to do, to be.

While all of us wish we could live our dreams, so few of us make the commitment to do what is necessary in order to achieve them. How lamentable. More about that when you turn the page, but for now what we care about is you. Grasp what it is that is important to you. In order to live the life you so deserve, recognize that your only true commitment is being true to yourself. You must, please, pay attention to trust and listen to the sure song of your heart, for it is the ecstatic notes that are the wondrous melody of manifestation. And makes the dream come alive.

Another thing. Borrowing Billy Shakespeare's masterpiece question, "To be or not to be?" demands that we be more than the questioner. It demands that we be, above all else, the quester, the inner traveler who bravely understands that empowerment and success is not an external path but an inner journey, what the Chinese call *nei kung*, a journey compassed in the soul and directed by the heart. So, once more, because it's important that you understand:

It's an inside job.

Be guided by what you feel. A tiger lives all of its days on earth with a committed heart and mind, a silent strength and stamina that speaks to all the world the dynamic truth that a tiger arrives at its mythic greatness by simply doing and being. You too must greet each daily dawning with the same resolve to experience the peace and joy of being fully alive. So, before you brush your teeth, with pure heart undertake the Pledge of Probability, the unequivocal oath of intense desire, the decisive decision that says YES to life and transforms all of your "I'd like to's into "I will."

Pledge that you intend to become the person you want to be. Make the commitment to be responsible for your dream. When you accept responsibility, you accept that you have the power of choice to do and to be. Zentrepreneurs know that when it comes to achieving success, the inner reservoir of commitment is the difference between a strong will and a strong won't. An encompassing presence, commitment contains an inner force of its own. Omnipotent and omnipresent, your strength will flow from this positive, resilient force that charges focus and desire into purposeful action. More than that, when you act with the deepest commitment, you act with enthusiasm and determination, a oneness of heart and mind that elevates your entire being to the highest level, calling up your great internal capacity to move with determined direction over, under, and around all doubt and circumstance, denying distractions and obstacles that may pull you from your path. Including commitment in your life, you are guided by what you feel and not by what you see. In other words, without any whisper of doubt, let commitment guide your every thought and every action. Every day.

Warning. Marching into commitment is not for the weak-willed or those with feet of clay. Despite what smiles and good luck the motivational golden gurus may send you on your way with to arrive at "I will do it!" know that you won't get so far so fast. Attention and circumstances will shift and alter. There will be pitfalls, brutal barriers unending. Know this: Commitment costs. When your prayer is to someday live your dream, there is a price to be paid. Being committed is not easy. Despite your best efforts, you will be hammered with the insidious hysteria of difficulties, disapproval, defeats, and disappointments, all of it, believe us, part of the treacherous terrain of the dream-seeking trail. But always remember this too: Commitment pays. Commitment is the magical potion that will transport you to the completion of what you start. Commitment means not allowing your destiny to be determined by fate, happenstance, or luck, but by conviction, stick-to-it-iveness, and, truth be told, toiling-hard work.

Desire + Decision + Determination = Success.

To commit is to have the strength and self-discipline to stay the course. To do. Absolutely. Much different and much stronger then the covenant of agreement, for when you agree to do something you provide yourself with the rationalizing wiggle room of keeping your agreement, changing your agreement, or canceling your agreement altogether. A commitment means you will do what needs to be done, no matter what. Real commitment is courage and perseverance. It is also the revelation of control, the process of assertion that lays claim that you are ready to affirm what you want and ready to do what it takes to acquire it. Commitment exudes optimism and self-confidence, the intensity of which can dispatch the pall of uncertainty, anxiety, and adversity—bags of burden that need to be lost. In the end, what's crucial to hold close is that commitment maintains supportive motivation and intensifies an indomitable will that will give you the empowerment to direct the course of your life, to create your future instead of allowing the future to create you. And that is essential.

Another Zen parable. Quick one. Promise.

A Zen monk and his student were walking along a river bank when the young student asked the master, "How will I know if what I seek is of the greatest importance?" The master abruptly took hold of the student and pulled him into the river, pushing the student's head fully under the water, continuing to hold the student there, despite the student's desperate thrashing, trying to free himself from the master's hold. Just at the perilous point of drowning, the master released his grip and the student surfaced, frantically gasping for air. "What were your thoughts as I held you under the water?" asked the master. "At the beginning 10,000 things," answered the student. "But in seconds, all that I could think of was air. I must do all that I can to get air!" "When you have that same intensity for what you desire," said the master, "you will make the commitment to what is of the greatest importance."

When intense desire becomes the air in your lungs, when you reach the point of wanting something with your whole being, determined to have it, willing to give your very all to it, you have arrived at the crossroads of commitment. The starting point for all success. You need only to claim (or reclaim) your dream. And then, oh then, take the one single splendid action that will secure such wonders. Take the relentless step of self-directedness.

Desire led and desire fed, commitment is what gives you the personal power to approach daily life with great faith in your original nature, your in-born tenacity to initiate and endure. Moving with your deepest desires, you become one with your inner tiger, determined and fearless, empowering yourself to overcome the confining circumstances imposed by others or those of your own making. While a tiger realizes it's the bars of a cage that holds it from being a tiger, man's enigma is that it is the space between the bars that keeps him from living his fullest life.

Now we want to stop here for a while and talk about what, as a condition, prevents so many, if not most, from taking that step, to constantly do what is necessary to exert the will, stay the course, and empower their dreams. What is it that can cripple so, what is the nature of their debilitating malady?

Simply stated, they are tragically and terribly, each and everyone of them, alas, ... paralyzed.

This isn't a typo. As these people live their lives they become more and more frozen, mentally handicapped by the trips and traps, the seed of negative conditioning that has perpetually plagued them and kept them from believing that they are deserving of success and fulfillment. We will refrain from all the psychobabble and just say that somewhere along their life journey, they have come to accept that someone else's opinion of them was more important than the opinion that they had of themselves. That what they wanted was inconsequential and that choice is not. That life can never be the way they want it to be. Stuck in the quagmire of self-doubts, unconscious patterns, and habitual habits, fearing the known and the unknown, perhaps because of letting the blather of others influence what they believe, they have lost belief in themselves, and with it their passion, their dream, ruefully denying their great capacity to live a life of wholeness and harmony, an existence of joy and grandeur.

A Zentrepreneur will have nothing to do with such limiting beliefs, agreeing with British statesman Benjamin Disraeli, who said, "Man is not a creature of circumstances. Circumstances are the creatures of man." And cheers to that. If your dream can be subjugated, then it was never your dream really. So if you ask what it will take to empower your dream, I will answer you in two words:

Courageous action.

Activate the force in your life. Creating a stalwart, dauntless attitude is the single most important ingredient in your recipe for success. Attitude leads to energy. Energy leads to strength. Strength leads to confidence. Confidence leads to courage. Courage leads to conviction. Conviction leads to commitment. And ultimately, your desires, your dreams ... your destiny.

The challenge, not too strong a word, is not to fall prey to procrastination, the mesmerizing effects of resistance, distraction, and fear. So here's something we know now that you soon will ... resistance, distraction, and fear, these are merely things that become visible when you take your eyes off your dream.

Make no mistake about this. When you let the thieves of resistance, distraction, and fear come along, shake you, and rob you of your attention, you create the reality that they exist. In other very important words, the only meaning that these things have is the meaning that you give them. Recognize these obstacles and deterrents as natural occurrences that always, always, challenge your focus, impede momentum, and dare to dissolve your discipline. The ruinous result—an excuse for inaction. Tragic. The abandonment of your plans and goals. More tragic yet. Your dreams set aside in abeyance, or, the greatest tragedy of all, forever given up on.

Do not abdicate your dream! You must not allow your attention to be distracted from what you desire or wish to be. Undivided attention is the key that will unlock the door to an abundant life. Hold fast to the unity of passion and purpose, your tiger heart and tiger mind, the expansive spirit of the powerful self, the dynamic that stirs and guides us all to the limitless possibilities within each of us. No need to retain the services of a mountain sherpa to take you to the roof of the world to seek the answer. Please, believe us, true enlightenment is just inches away. Between your ears you carry the essential perspective and energy to recognize the truth, to see things for what they are. Know that resistance is the gravitational pull of the past or a myopic view of the future. Distractions will pull you here or take you there. Fear wants you to stay in the comfy cozy safety of where you are. It takes a great amount of hanging in, derring-do, to move forward and see through these attention-grabbing, passion-pilfering diversions. And think it's easy? Good luck.

Get ready now, here comes some words Ron and I want you to glance over.

Certitude

Resolve

Determination

Passion

Conviction

Drive

Intensity

Steadfast

Deliberate

Verve

Purpose

Unwavering

Intent

Fervor

Will

Discipline

Certainty

Persistence

Control

Passion (Yes, we know we already mentioned passion but it's important enough to mention again.)

Dedication

Constancy

Fortitude

Spunk

Tenacity

Unshakable

Grit

Belief

Endurance

Question for you. What do these words represent to you? Go ahead and glance again. We'll wait.

Okay, got your answer? Save it. Here's the answer we want: Know that these words represent promise or pitfall. Up to you. They are the connective word-stock of the heart and spirit that condition the wondrous capacity of your mind to accept the fact that only an ongoing, deep-seated commitment to your goals and dreams will deliver you to experience an ecstatic life.

Seven days without commitment make one weak.

A strong mind is capable of holding a strong thought, which can fill your entire being as tea fills a cup. An example here that may be useful to remember is that masters of the Japanese tea ceremony are imbued with the term *kokoro ire*, or embodiment of the heart spirit. For more than four hundred and fifty years, the honored sanctity of the tea ceremony is the result of the host's whole being being dedicated to the preparation for a tea gathering, executing the role with sincere heart, spirit, and mind. A competence that's inspired and inspiring. Fill your heart, your spirit, and your mind with the same determined concentration, and allow life to live you. Dedicate yourself to travel the distance. Buddha said that the only mistake one can make along the road to truth is not going all the way. Confucius said that it matters not what we try, what matters is that once we begin, we must never lose heart until the task is completed. The inability to live your dream is simply an inability to stay committed. Remember, again, that turning your dream into a reality is, and always will be, crucially and truly, a concentrated task.

It's an inside job.

So moving on, take the responsibility to accomplish and attain. Transform the inert energy of aspiration into the active energy of commitment. Focus with ferocity on being what you want to be, doing what you want to do, and having what you want to have. Cultivate commitment comfortably inside you. Commitment is passion, held steady by will. It is, as we have said, almost everything. Be skilled at bringing a full consciousness to mastering the transforming oneness of a consecrated mind. The authentic Zentrepreneur subscribes to the notable realization: One moon shines in every pond—in every pond the one moon. More than anything else, a Zentrepreneur's obligation is to become one with the sublime power of an empowered mind.

For your mind, like the future, is only what you make of it.

Chapter Nine
JOURNEY FORWARD

TRAVELING WITHIN,
TRAVELING WITHOUT

Even in mythology, a backwards tiger does not exist.

Essential truism. You can't let go into the future if you can't let go of the past.

The not-so-remarkable reason is that it takes a dedicated focus of energy to empower your dream. Energy focused primarily on positive thoughts and events, dedicated toward the constructive and the creative, has the power to transcend us, moving beyond the ordinary. Believe it to be unquestionably true that inner energy is the force that can transform outer change, shaping our world and everything in it.

It's unfortunate that so many grasp on to everything that has happened to them as if their lives depended on it, when in fact, the great glory of life depends on letting go. Ralph Waldo Emerson said that you must let go of a thing for a new one to come to you. Sage advice. By jettisoning certain embraced emotions, you make way to receive more of the innate joy life has for you. Detach yourself from grudge and grievances. Holding on to bitterness, you will satisfy no one. Let go of old hurts, unkind words, broken promises, the scrapes and scars inflicted by friends, loved ones, and past relationships. These are vitriolic voids that pilfer and pulverize energy.

Include them out.

Painful memories, fault-finding, and unhappy feelings sap enormous energy and contribute to making you feel unworthy and undeserving. Holding judgments against others, we are actually holding back ourselves, impeding our journey forward. When you allow your energy to be channeled in the direction of rancor, to expend even the smallest amount of it to cling to unresolved emotions such as anger, resentment, hostility, disappointment, guilt, or envy, is to obstruct the flow of vital energy needed to cultivate and deliver empowerment. But be warned. There is no empowerment without undeviating focused energy. Again, holding on will hold you back. Animosity, complaint, and resentment deter precious energy and poison the air. This is why so many dreams die somewhere along the way.

Use your energy to be pre-active rather than reactive. To direct your energy is to direct your destiny. Guard against allowing unconsciously conditioned emotions that will wear you down and drain you from empowering your dream. Not to do so is to embrace sabotaging behavior, an excuse for inaction that will dominate your time and squander your success. Take care to realize that by not abandoning such feelings, you end up abandoning your self. By blaming someone else for your circumstance you put them in charge of your life, relinquishing control of your destiny. This is unallowable and ruinous. Having the valiancy to move past the negative feelings of ill-will toward others who may have wronged you in life is to have the power to manifest true miracle-making.

The Zentrepreneur believes the teacher is everywhere. No matter how hurtful an experience, accept everybody and everything as they are; regard those individuals who have angered you or have caused resentment as teachers who entered your life for a purpose. Make the decision to journey forward, looking back upon them as providing lessons learned about how you can better shape your own attitudes, actions, and behaviors and go beyond. Benjamin Franklin said, "Those things that hurt, instruct." In fact, all experience contains a valuable manifesting lesson. Every encounter has something to teach.

Resolve to reclaim empowering energy through forgiveness, and as a result, attain peace and freedom in the process. Affirm the belief that forgiveness facilitates by allowing increased energy to come in. Once again with a tip of the hat to Emerson, in order to bring more into your life, let more out of it. It was also Emerson who said that for every minute you are angry, you lose sixty seconds of happiness. Hear, hear.

The Zentrepreneurs' duty is not to attach the blame for the past, rather their duty is to attach the way for the future. The decision to let go brings relief and release, freeing up vibrant, achieving action to act on the things that are important in your life. Zentrepreneurs live a life of grace without gravity. For them, Sir Isaac Newton and his up-and-down apple revelation have no meaning. The Zentrepreneur lives in an entirely different realm, not weighted down by the past.

Never permit your time, vitality, and emotional energy to be used to continue maintaining a past tense. Forgiveness frees the forgiver. Empty your mind of negative memories and their embraced impact, so it can fill with new understanding. The point to all of this is that to linger in the past is to do so at the expense of your future. You must come to realize that the people, places, and circumstances of your past are not ultimately responsible for your being happy or unhappy. It is your investment in either of them that determines a joyful life. A Zentrepreneur can overcome any attachment by leaving it behind. There is no way that someone writing a book like this can help you in a psychiatric, laying-on-a-couch sort of way, other than to simply suggest that when you let go of all meaning, only what's truly important becomes meaningful.

Your happiness.

The poets tell us that we always have a choice, and that we alone are responsible for what is chosen. The wise Zentrepreneur knows that energy goes wherever it is focused, and the more energy that is focused on what is important, the better the choices we will make. Which brings us now to the most important choice of all, the magnificent decision to journey forward. But before we begin, a word about what to bring along with. Actually two words:

Heart and mind.

That's it. That's all you need. Within your tiger heart and tiger mind, you carry the real power that can and will guide you on the step-by-step process to genuine joy. For empowering a dream is not a journey of destination, it is a process where each step forward depends upon the step that was taken before. By allowing your spiritual tiger to transcend, you will travel the sure-footed way of the tiger, not recognizing any obstacle as a deterrent from what you seek. Not easily dissuaded, a tiger turns right or it turns left, or it simply walks over an obstacle. If there is no way for itself, walking with confidence and clarity of intent, it makes one. A tiger simplifies its journey by doing no more or no less, than deciding on going where it wishes to be.

A trait that you too must hold dear.

Make the decision to never, ever let anything stop you from obtaining what you want in life. Journey the field of boundless possibility by deciding that your life is not shaped by your past, but by your decision to choose a life dedicated to what is worthy of your time, attention, and energy. Your passionate pursuit. Create your own condition of consciousness and accept the responsibility for shaping your attitudes and aspirations. When you awaken the tiger way within, you release a reservoir of infinite potential. Setting aside any doubts or thoughts that interfere, you immerse yourself in the present, focusing whole energy and all of your emotional resources to overcome whatever inner obstructions stand in the way of who you are and what you yearn to do. Now we're not saying that this is glorious, gifted guidance: There is no finger-pointing research that exists for any of this. It's just the difference between a life of dreaming and a life of doing.

And always will be.

Chapter Ten
LIVING A TIGER'S LIFE

WILL AND GRACE

A tiger walks the earth not with the sun in its eyes,

but with the sun in its heart.

Because strange forces shape our lives, the not-so-surprising surprise is that at this time in our history, we all live in a country in which today—right now—the most popular genre in publishing is ... roll of drums, please ... the self-help book. There are many millions of these motivational mantras being sold and for those would-be wordsmiths out there ready to sing the same song, for reasons known only to science, a booming business awaits.

But what is important for you to understand about those books, the much coveted titles, at least many of them, well at least this one, is that there is no right methodology. There is only what moves you. To act. To do. To be.

The players of the field include Norman Vincent Peale, Napoleon Hill, Zig Ziglar, Dale

Carnegie, plus Stephen Covey, plus, plus Tony Robbins, and let's toss into this mix the likes of Cheryl Richardson and Dr. Phil—adding it up, we're none of us curing cancer. The operative truth is that we are all mostly merchants of our ideas and our ideas, merely the merchandise. In other very important words: Buyer beware.

Despite the shelves being stuffed with many a title promising a frothy skip into the sunset with lasting bliss, conjuring a meaningful, congruent course of action is up to you to determine for yourself. To allow yourself to open your psychological space to follow the bounce and drive of any quick-fix idea is not only madness, it is to weep. Hopefully the point that has come clearer into focus these many pages is (and put this in huge caps):

IT IS YOU WHO HAS TO RISE ABOVE WHATEVER INSECURITIES OR BELIEFS YOU ASSUME RENDERS YOU INCAPABLE OF LIVING AN INTENTIONAL LIFE.

It's as cut and dried as that.

Here is the unpolished truth: You cannot buy a rainbow and climb up to the sky. There is no simple five steps to this or seven rules of that. There's a certain heaviness to happiness that is not so easily lifted. Empowering your dream is mainly, a tremendously toiling task, like arthritically picking up Jello. Decisions to direct your inner strength, your energy, and focus toward mindsets and activities that can make a measurable difference in reaching your goals, incorporating doing what needs to be done the sum and substance of your daily life, is the pick and shovel that will initiate the transformation you desire. Buddha said, "Believe nothing," no matter where you read it, or who said it, unless it agrees with your own reason. Emerson said, "To believe what is true for you in your private heart is genius." No matter what the course, system, or strategy, you must rely upon yourself. Regardless of what any book beckons, please believe that the path to achieving your deserved greatness cannot be taught, it must be taken.

Sociologists take note, as we now repeat something that we touched on earlier in this book. Because it bears repeating. To live a dream is not some rare reservoir inhabited by only certain races, religions, or genders, or the cultured few, or those who are more gifted, luckier, or more advantaged.

To live a life of gladness, all any of us has to do is reclaim our personal power and take charge of our lives, affirming our boundless belief in our potential to succeed. It's decisions, not conditions, that empower our dream. A Zentrepreneur lives by choice, not by chance.

Back to the business at hand. The thing that has been changing the turf, what has made the self-help books darlings is, of course, simple and obvious. People are looking for answers. Constantly. So is the shame. For too much of life is spent on looking for the right answers, when the secret to life lies in being able to ask the right questions. It is the questions we ask or fail to ask that shape our path. Look beyond the words of others and look for meaning that inspires and motivates you, reawakening your own inner realization. And while those other tomes busy themselves with telling you what you need to do with your life, this is a Zentrepreneur's Guide with only one crucial proviso, to demand that you *do* with your life.

There is the difference—pure and simple.

Ron and I know nothing, but we think this: The one true power that you absolutely have is the power to make yourself happy. All of the time. Accept the responsibility for creating your own experience. Awaken yourself to new insights, sensitivities, and possibilities, identifying with the joy of life that is yours to pursue ecstatically and lay claim to. Happiness does not exist in outer circumstances, it exists within the following of your own blissful nature. Discover your *chen tao*, what the Chinese call the "correct path," realizing that while there is no right path, there exists a path that is right for you. Begin by asking yourself the right questions. By right questions, are the questions meaningful, do they come from the heart— are they capable of leading you to where you want to go? Questions create and transform, allowing you to develop and acquire intelligence, teaching, that in the end, the answer is always found in the question.

The thing that we're trying to emphasize is this: Zentrepreneur Guides don't ask you to become something you're not, but ask that you become more fully what you are. Allowing your inner tiger is something to be lived rather than studied, since study can only take you part of the way. And while no words of any book can make it true, understanding that you create your own reality can make it so.

I have believed that for a long time and still do.

Get down to the heart of the matter. Seek clarity and insight asking what is it that turns you on and soars your soul? Where is it that your capacities want you to go? What is it that you want to ultimately experience and succeed at? In order to create outer movement in your life, you must turn inward. Look within. Get to know the knower. Dust yourself off and get in touch with the real you. The person who takes a noggin-knock and suffers amnesia doesn't become another person—the person simply loses touch with who he or she is. Have the willingness to deeply re-examine and re-imagine your life, re-connecting with your passion, your unique visions, your innate instincts, talents, and gifts. Doubt not the freshness your encounter will bring, the hue of new hope that will materialize. Just as nature insists that green is the color of awakening, re-emerging from winter snows without fail, so too is the appearance of instinctive rightness. Because you never really stop dreaming your dream, part of you doesn't, anyway.

Awaken the sleeper. Recognize your own original nature. Rediscover your passion and will. Listen for your inner urging drumbeat. Get to your possibilities. Get to your purpose. Simply put: Get in touch. Take the time to do so.

Now.

Do not delay and put this off. Take a serious break from the speed of life and bring into being this imperative encounter. Socrates said, "Know thyself." The best advice. Get up close and personal. It's very important that you take the time to do this. Please. This is a big deal. A very big deal. This is you we're talking about.

As an exercise, however hauntingly, contemplatively spend more than a moment looking in the mirror. Out of light and shadow, infiltrate your internal government. Take in what comes up on your inner screen. Let the mirror throw back true reflection. Is the image you're making the image you see? Are you who you want to be? If not, why not? Wait. Before you answer, letting madness make its entrance—I'm not rich enough or I've got too many responsibilities—know that to live a love-what-you-do life, no obstacle is insurmountable. If you are not living such a life, then no compensation is adequate. The ancient Zen masters cautioned that the more coins you carry in your pocket, the more the coins will weigh you down. Concern yourself not with how much money you are making, concern yourself, instead, with what the money is making of you.

Reclaim your bliss!

But be warned, the path of a Zentrepreneur is an expensive journey. You pay by giving up the familiar, the bloat and banishment of predictability and everyday sameness. To travel where your passion and potential take you, to accept what you want to do over what others say you should do, is to accept that there's more to life than Visa card payments. To partake in infinity, it doesn't take a dollar more or a dollar less. All it takes is that you become clearly aware that the inner process of self-mastery is immanent, waiting for you to empower your best life. Remembering that Zentrepreneurs cultivate and hold dear to what is within, to what they are without.

Implicitly.

Well, dear readers, this is as far as we get to go. But, before closing up shop, here, is the fact. The Zentrepreneur, like the tiger, inhabits the profound principles of harmony, wholeness, and balance. A living flame of will and grace that is both penetrating and protecting, a limitless spirit that demands to be honored. As we have at times so tragically seen, the wild tiger is not the be-whiskered, cuddly, kitty-pie creature that the Disney drawers would have you believe. Forget that at your peril. They are ethereal beasts of untamable strength and natural instinct, magisterial beings with inexhaustible aggressive energies that can spontaneously rise up to deliver the fullest potential of their natural life. They are at all times what they naturally were meant to be.

And so are you.

The test is: Will you choose to recognize your tiger heart and tiger mind? That's the pulse of this book we hope you take along with, an urging for you to achieve a higher consciousness, to radiate your vital inner pool of empowerment, embracing your decision-making power not to settle for anything less than experiencing an existence of beauty. Living the tiger life is to be, in the end, a chooser of roads, to bravely venture into the dark wood of uncertainty, having the essential courage and intemperate passion to live by, consciously and deliberately setting your own direction. To walk the pathless path is to wake up every green morning and undertake the Zentrepreneurial journey. Having the faith to find your own way, undaunted, unbowed, never yielding to doubt, this is the crucial and glorious thing.

The magic life.

There's a revered Zen koan about a student who asked his master, "No matter what lies ahead, what is the Way?" The master quickly replied, "The Way is your daily life." And so it is. To empower your dream is deeply nothing more than living every day of the world, believing in your true self. Making the biology of self-belief part of your organic makeup, your glowing persona, understanding that believing in yourself is a condition of the heart and mind and not a list of things to perform will deliver you to the splendor of your deserved greatness. Please be alive to the idea that the glory of your dream can and will happen. All you need do is to only, and for always, believe in the potential and the promise of the essential you. After all, someone has to believe in the believer.

To which we say finally, and most of all:

We will if you will.

Wishing you everything good, true, and beautiful....

EPILOGUE

Thank you for the taking of your time to read our book. It is our impassioned hope that you will dedicate yourself to continuing to travel the Zentrepreneur journey, where each step further delivers you to living an empowered life. Please come back to visit these pages again and again, knowing that they will keep fresh and bring deeper meaning each time. As we have in other Zentrepreneur Guides®, we would like to leave you with the noble task of reading one new book each and every week, for reading the right books, exposing yourself to new ideas and insights, can be the key to unlocking a life of happiness and fulfillment. Invest in yourself, buy into the absolute that the reading of books will renew your essence and empower your dreams. Start by considering the following titles. Though the list we offer up may appear to be long, we would like you to remember it's not how many of the books that you are able to get through that matters, what really matters is how many of the books are able to get through to you.

—*Ron Rubin*

Book List

For starters:

Wowisms: Words of Wisdom for Dreamers and Doers,
   by Ron Rubin and Stuart Avery Gold

Dragon Spirit: How to Self-Market Your Dream,
   by Ron Rubin and Stuart Avery Gold

Success at Life: How to Catch and Live Your Dream,
   by Ron Rubin and Stuart Avery Gold

The Republic of Tea: How an Idea Becomes a Business,
   by Mel Ziegler, Patricia Ziegler,
   and Bill Rosenzweig

Re-imagine: Business Excellence in a Disruptive Age,
   by Tom Peters

*Stand Up for Your Life: A Practical Step-by-Step Plan to
   Build Inner Confidence and Personal Power*,
   by Cheryl Richardson

Purple Cow: Transform Your Business by Being Remarkable,
   by Seth Godin

*The New Culture of Desire: The Pleasure Imperative Trans-
   forming Your Business and Your Life*,
   by Melinda Davis

How to Make Big Money in Your Own Small Business,
> by Jeffrey J. Fox

The Fall of Advertising and the Rise of PR,
> by Al Ries and Laura Ries

Do It Anyway: The Handbook for Finding Personal
> *Meaning and Deep Happiness in a Crazy World,*
> by Kent M. Keith

The Right Questions: Ten Essential Questions to Guide You
> *to an Extraordinary Life,*
> by Debbie Ford

I Don't Know What I Want, but I Know It's Not This: A
> *Step-by-Step Guide to Finding Gratifying Work,*
> by Julie Jansen

Second Acts: Creating the Life You Really Want, Building
> *the Career You Truly Desire,*
> by Stephen M. Pollan and Mark Levine

What Color Is Your Parachute,
> by Richard Nelson Bolles

There Must be MORE than This: Finding More Life, Love,
> *and Meaning by Overcoming Your Soft Addictions,*
> by Judith Wright

Instructions to the Cook: A Zen Master's Lessons in Living a
        Life that Matters,
        by Rick Fields and Bernard Glassman

Attracting Perfect Customers: The Power of Strategic
        Synchronicity,
        by Stacey Hall and Jan Brogniez

One Day, All Children: The Unlikely Story of Teach for
        America and What I Learned Along the Way,
        by Wendy Kopp

Trading Up: The New American Luxury,
        by Michael J. Silverstein and Neil Fiske

What Should I Do with My Life: The True Story of People
        Who Answered the Ultimate Question,
        by Po Bronson

American Still Life: The Jim Beam Story and the Making of
        the World's #1 Bourbon,
        by F. Paul Pacult

Marketing Insights from A to Z: 80 Concepts Every
        Manager Needs to Know,
        by Philip Kotler

Just Ask a Woman: Cracking the Code of What Women
        Want and How They Buy,
        by Mary Lou Quinlan

Thinking for a Change: 11 Ways Highly Successful People Approach Life and Work,
by John C. Maxwell

Capital Instincts: Life as an Entrepreneur, Financier, and Athlete,
by Richard L. Brandt with contributions by Thomas Weisel

Marketing to Women: How to Understand, Reach, and Increase Your Share of the World's Largest Market Segment,
by Martha Barletta

Dictionary of the FUTURE: The Words, Terms and Trends That Define the Way We'll Live, Work and Talk,
by Faith Popcorn and Adam Hanft

Take Yourself To The Top: The Secrets of America's # 1 Career Coach,
by Laura Berman Fortgang

The Tipping Point: How Little Things Can Make a Big Difference,
by Malcom Gladwell

At Home in the Muddy Water: The Zen of Living with Everyday Chaos,
by Ezra Bayda

Tao The Watercourse Way,
   by Allan W. Watts

Everyday Zen: Love and Work,
   by Charlotte J. Beck

Life's Greatest Lessons: 20 Things that Matter,
   by Hal Urban

Lao Tzu: Tao Te Ching: A Book about the Way and The Power of the Way,
   by Ursula K. Le Guin

The Power of Myth,
   by Joseph Campbell

Execution: The Discipline of Getting Things Done,
   by Ram Charan, Charles Burck, and
   Larry Bossidy

The Little Engine That Could,
   by Watty Piper

Optimal Thinking: How to Be Your Best Self,
   by Rosalene Glickman

How to Practice: The Way to a Meaningful Life,
   by the Dalai Lama

The Power of Now: A Guide to Spiritual Enlightenment,
   by Eckhart Tolle

Acknowledgments

A trillion, zillion thanks to the publishers and readers across the world who have taken the translations of Zentrepreneur Guides into their hearts and souls.

To Zentrepreneurs, past, present and future for daring to chance.

To Pam, Julie and Todd. To Andy, Aaryn, and Shaun. Always...always...always.

To Julian B. Venezky, who at 95 years young shows up ready for work each and every day.

To Gina Amador whose design continues to capture the art of perfection time after time.

To Machiko for her inks and paints and storied tiger drawings. Her energy and imagination brought spirit to this book.

To Fauzia Burke for her boisterous buzz.

To everyone at Newmarket Press for their enthusiasm and get-it-done diligence, especially for the wisdom and clarity of Keith Hollaman and the fabulous without-fail support of Paul Sugarman, Shannon Berning, Harry Burton, Heidi Sachner, Frank DeMaio, and to William Rusin and Dosier Hammond of W.W. Norton & Company.

And gratitude beyond measure to Esther Margolis, our publisher and prodder, who helps us see new light at those times when we feel that there is none.

About the Authors

Ron Rubin bought and took charge of The Republic of Tea in 1994, a two-year-old company that had been founded by the same people who created The Banana Republic. Shortly thereafter, marketing veteran **Stuart Avery Gold** joined Rubin in the company's mission to create a Tea Revolution. In keeping with its whimsical identity as an independent nation, The Republic of Tea calls its employees Ministers, its customers Citizens, and its sales outlets Embassies. Ron Rubin, the "Minister of Tea," is Chairman of the Board. Stuart Avery Gold, the "Minister of Travel," is COO and the company editorial "voice." Ron Rubin resides in Clayton, Missouri, and Stuart Avery Gold lives in Boca Raton, Florida.

The Republic of Tea headquarters are located in Novato, California. *The Republic of Tea* sells the finest teas and herbs in the world to specialty food and select department stores, cafés, and restaurants and through its award-winning mail order catalog and Website: **www.republicoftea.com.**

In 2001, the authors published their first volume, *Success at Life: How to Catch and Live Your Dream*, in the acclaimed Zentrepreneur Guide® series, which now also includes *Dragon Spirit: How to Self-Market Your Dream, Wowisms: Words of Wisdom for Dreamers and Doers,* and *Tiger Heart, Tiger Mind: How to Empower Your Dream.*

Zentrepreneur Guide® books are about dreaming and doing, an opportunity to present a path of power that will allow you to create for yourself a success at life that reflects who you truly are. They are about being guided by an inner-wind that can transport you to a place and time where your dreams can and will come true.

Ultimately, it is about the joy-filled destiny you can and must shape for yourself by embracing dreaming and being. That said, it pleases us to invite you to let go of the nightmarish unreality of the reality that has hold of you and give yourself over to the splendor of the dream waiting to have you. It is as simple and as exciting as that.

You will find tantalizing excerpts from some of our other titles on the following pages. Enjoy!

Excerpt from *Wowisms*

You must commit yourself fully to manifesting your ability. But understand that wanting to will not be enough. Willing to will not be enough. There is no will or want, there is only to do. You must do in order to master the circumstances of life or risk having the circumstances of life master you.

From *Wowisms: Words of Wisdom for Dreamers and Doers.*
Copyright ©2003 by Ron Rubin and Stuart Avery Gold

Excerpts from *Success at Life*

Zentrepreneurs have unconditional self-regard. Trusting his or her own instincts, they spend little or no time thinking about what they can't do and instead think entirely in terms of what they *can* and *must* do to catch and live their dreams.

A Zentrepreneur exercises joy and sincerity, promotes illumination, and actively seeks inspiration and gives inspiration to others. He or she shares wisdom, moving toward ever-greater harmony and balance, energizing others with their own enthusiasm.

Zentrepreneurs enchant their lives with confidence and hope, realizing that they have the energy to cope with circumstances, and that they also possess the power to generate new possibilities of thought and action.

Zentrepreneurs deal with events directly and clearly, managing their minds with flexibility and managing their bodies with calmness.

A Zentrepreneur gravitates towards positive people and situations, seeking out those who will support and inspire, cutting away from those who discourage, distract or undermine.

A Zentrepreneur knows that to move on, sometimes the best light for the journey can be the result of a burning bridge.

Zentrepreneurs are spiritual human beings making time to celebrate the beauty and the mystery of life. They recognize the creative intelligence of the universe and respect the interdependent synchronicity of all things. If a butterfly flaps its wings in Japan, a breeze can be felt in the Caribbean. Everything is connected. The nineteenth-century naturalist John Muir said, "When we tug at a single thing in nature we find that it is attached to the rest of the world." Zentrepreneurs embrace the process of life, allowing themselves to be taken with the spiritual energies of the universe, knowing that they too are part of the unity of all things.

• • •

Albert Einstein, who was only smarter than all of us, said, "You cannot solve a problem with the same consciousness that created it." To underscore, a recent study of Fortune 500 CEO's found that these successful people relied upon set-aside periods in their daily schedules for quiet reflection. The sheer busyness of business requires, demands, this need for a clear space. They reported that some sort of centering meditative exercise was essential for them to reconnect with their intuition and inspiration, allowing them to think clearly and insightfully, helping them to make more effective decisions. Chuang Tzu noted that when people wish to see their reflections, they do not look into running water, they look into still water. By allocating time with themselves *for* themselves, they are able to achieve a personal transcendence that nourishes and exercises mental and spiritual well-being. This effecting of both an outer and an inner fitness has helped them to find the wisdom of the real bottom line:

A healthy mind and body is the true incontestable currency of success.

Now there is a lesson to be learned through this example, actually two. The first is, that one great piece of advice is something we should all be grateful for. And the second: In order to become a success at life and live your dream, understand that you must take care of your gifts.

Pleeease take care of your gifts.

From Chapter Four: "Risk," and Chapter Eight: "Secrets of the Temple," from *Success at Life: How to Catch and Live Your Dream.*
Copyright ©2001 by Ron Rubin and Stuart Avery Gold

Excerpts from *Dragon Spirit*

And follow your heart.

There are certain absolute truths on this planet and one of them is that the mind can play tricks, but the heart cannot be fooled. The thirteenth-century Sufi poet Rumi said, "Everyone has been made for some particular work and the desire for that work has been put in every heart." While questions, confusion, fear, and doubt are merely mental, the answers for all that is true reside in the purposeful whispers of the heart. Only when your eyes are wide open to this realization will you see the light of choice. Only when you silence the vacillation and confusion of the mind can you hear the voice of your heart. And experience the process through which each one of us comes to discover the conscious contact with our source. Believe in the great idea for your life, knowing that there is an idea for every time and a time for every idea. Ideas are only as unique as the individual that it attaches itself to. While some make the mistake of wasting time and money on the process of positioning an idea in the marketplace, others understand that success comes from the process of positioning themselves.

Understand ideas are opportunities. Nothing more, nothing less. Pregnant with promise, teeming with potential, they are fluid and adaptive, waiting to be brought to fruition, a catalyst for transformation that pulls and urges forward, allowing for the kind of dream delivering we need so much on Earth these days. First and last, they are serendipitous openings for glory and joy, waiting for that certain individual whose unique time it is to deliver it out of the darkness, but for now what we care about is you.

So here's the one final thing we want you to know . . .
It's always your time.

• • •

Remember daily that self-marketing your dream is not a problem to be solved, but a reality to be lived.

Focus your behavior on activities that nourish, strengthen, and harmonize the whole of your well-being.

Because again, wellness matters.

As does joy. As does serenity and happiness. The unspoken tragedy is that a growing number believe that harmony and gladness exist for them somewhere far beyond the edges of their time-bound world. Not so. Bliss and contentment is there for us if we would only be there for it. While we all live distracted by a world blurred by disturbance, there is nothing that cannot be gotten rid off, no burden that cannot be lifted, no care that cannot be dissolved, by taking the time to experience the life that is in front of us. Awaken yourself. Slow down. Be grateful. And then, oh then, take notice of the marvel, the perfection, the natural serenity, and the true esthetic in every moment and every thing that daily life offers.

While an entrepreneur creates a business, a Zentrepreneur creates a business and a life.

This is the Zentrepreneur's highest mandate. And the absolute golden rule.

From Chapter Ten: "Follow Your Bliss," and Chapter Eleven: "Prepare Yourself," from *Dragon Spirit: How to Empower Your Dream.*
Copyright ©2003 by Ron Rubin and Stuart Avery Gold

SHARE THE JOURNEY

Tell us your story

As the proud publisher of this book, we hope that you have been inspired to discover the Zentrepreneur in you. The fact that you purchased this book proves that you are open to your limitless potential. If someone gave you this book it proves that someone recognizes your limitless potential. We invite you to share with us your thoughts and experiences about becoming a Zentrepreneur. The best contributors and their stories may even be used in future Zentrepreneur Guides®.

Keep up-to-date

If you'd like to stay abreast of Zentrepreneur Guide publications and activities, join our mailing list (we don't sell or pass on mailing list information). See below for where to send your name and email or address.

All Zentrepreneur Guide correspondence should be sent to

> Zentrepreneur Guides
> Newmarket Press
> 18 E. 48th Street
> New York, NY 10017

Ron and Stuart can be reached at **www.zentrepreneurs.com**.